100
TRAINING
GAMES

100
TRAINING GAMES

GARY KROEHNERT

McGRAW-HILL BOOK COMPANY Sydney

New York San Francisco Auckland Bogotá Caracas
Lisbon London Madrid Mexico City Milan Montreal
New Delhi San Juan Singapore Tokyo Toronto

National Library of Australia
Cataloguing-in-Publication data:
Kroehnert, Gary.
  100 training games.

  Bibliography.
  ISBN 0 07 452770 3.

  1. Employees—Training of—Simulation methods. 2. Management games. I. Title. II. Title: One hundred training games.

658.3124

Produced in Australia by Oldstyle Publishing Services for
  McGraw-Hill Book Company Australia Pty Limited
  4 Barcoo Street, Roseville, NSW 2069
Typesetting processed in Australia by Everysize Typeart Services
Printed in Hong Kong by Dah Hua Printing Press Co. Ltd

Publisher: James O'Toole
Production Editor: Margaret Olds
Designer: Kim Webber
Illustrators: Maria Mason and Kim Webber

CONTENTS

INTRODUCTION 7
THE ACTIVITIES 9
GAMES CODES GRID 14

THE GAMES 17

No.	Name	Page	No.	Name	Page
1.	Too Many Solutions?	18	24.	Put Your Jacket On	55
2.	Relay	19	25.	Light Your Cigarette	56
3.	Human Machines	20	26.	Stepping In	57
4.	Garage Sale	21	27.	Manipulation	58
5.	Clear the Deck	22	28.	What Do People Want?	59
6.	New Ideas	24	29.	Capital Punishment	61
7.	I Am …	25	30.	The Word Game	63
8.	Telling Lies	27	31.	Spelling Bee	65
9.	AAA of Stress Management	28	32.	Another Spelling Bee	67
10.	Introductions	30	33.	Team Task No. 1	69
11.	Signatures	32	34.	Team Task No. 2	71
12.	Join the Dots	33	35.	3-Minute Test	73
13.	Brain Teasers	38	36.	Pass the Microphone	75
14.	Scavenger Hunt	40	37.	The Watch Face	76
15.	Brainstorm Destruction	42	38.	Relaxation	77
16.	Action Plans	43	39.	Note to Me	78
17.	Stretch Monitor	45	40.	The Numbers Game	79
18.	Tied in Knots	46	41.	Puppets	81
19.	Common Words	47	42.	No Laughing	82
20.	What's Your Name?	49	43.	Shuffling Papers	83
21.	Beans	50	44.	Cleaning Up	84
22.	Pass It On	52	45.	What Do You See?	85
23.	Building Blocks	54	46.	Smile	87

No.	Name	Page		No.	Name	Page
47.	Stress Budget	89		74.	Faces	135
48.	Negotiation	90		75.	Follow-up to Murphy's Law	137
49.	Our Greatest Fears	91		76.	Them and Us	139
50.	Marooned	93		77.	The Brainstorm	141
51.	Signs	94		78.	Clasp Your Hands	142
52.	Balloon Ball	96		79.	Fold Your Arms	143
53.	Tortoise, Hare or Thoroughbred	97		80.	Clowns	144
54.	Where Are We Now?	99		81.	What's My Object?	146
55.	Overcoming Fear	100		82.	Come Back	147
56.	Memory Test	102		83.	Post-it	148
57.	Say What?	104		84.	15 Pieces	149
58.	Room 703	105		85.	Housie	151
59.	List of Names	107		86.	Participant Bingo	152
60.	Folding Paper	108		87.	Pick a Shape	154
61.	Learning by Linking	109		88.	2-Minute Talk	156
62.	What Is It?	112		89.	Where Did It Go?	157
63.	Circuit Overload	114		90.	Post Me a Note	159
64.	Tangrams	116		91.	Spider's Web	160
65.	In-Tray	119		92.	Personally	161
66.	tebahplA ehT	120		93.	The Application	162
67.	How's Your Memory?	122		94.	Clap	163
68.	Tennis Balls	124		95.	Time Line	164
69.	Having Fun	126		96.	Orientation Quiz	165
70.	My Worries	128		97.	People Scavenger	166
71.	Moon Explorer Problem	130		98.	Co-operation	168
72.	Fall-out Shelter	132		99.	Paper Planes	169
73.	A Case of Labelling	134		100.	Agenda	171

SAMPLE OBSERVER'S SHEETS   172
BIBLIOGRAPHY AND OTHER REFERENCES   176

INTRODUCTION

We have all seen and probably participated in various forms of training games, simulations, role-plays, brain teasers, case studies and other related activities. Just because we are aware of them doesn't mean that we can use them any time we wish to.

The use of these activities should allow the participant to discover outcomes, rather than be told everything without trying it. Most of the world's airlines, manufacturing plants, human resource companies, military establishments, small and large companies, private and public organizations now use these forms of structured exercises. The ultimate goal should always be improved learning.

What these trainers and participants are generally interested in, on top of the information sessions, are structured experiences that they can apply, where no one feels terribly threatened or where they don't have to touch strangers. The other very important criterion that almost everyone agrees on is that the experience should be relevant to the training matter or relevant to the group requirements.

All facilitators using structured exercises need to be aware that other things may come out in the use of games that normally wouldn't come out using other methods of instruction.

Games, simulations, role-plays, brain teasers, case studies and other related activities have been used successfully in innumerable training situations for many centuries by countless numbers of trainers. We can actually trace the use of games and simulations back thousands of years. Chess is an excellent example of this.

For most of us, games, simulations and role-plays were part of the growing-up process. From our earliest school days, we remember playing games such as marbles or hide-and-go-seek. It is now recognized that these games are not only for fun, but also prepare the child for entry into the social system. If any of you took Home Economics, Woodwork or Metalwork at school, you would probably call them a simulation of the real workplace. Some of us may also remember acting out roles in a game of 'Mothers and Fathers'—another form of role-play.

In a training situation we must be very selective in the use and timing of these methods of instruction. People become bored doing the same thing all the time, even if it is a 'mind-blowing experience' the first few times. If you intend using these methods effectively, plan them into your session notes or your outline.

This book is aimed at giving new trainers enough information, samples and sources to competently carry out their function as adult trainers. It focuses primarily on games and brain teasers, as role-plays and case studies have to be designed by the individual trainer for each separate application. For new trainers I would strongly suggest that they also spend some time looking at my training handbook titled *Basic Training for Trainers* (McGraw-Hill Book Company Australia, 1990).

Today's trainer can simply walk down to the local shopping center and purchase any number of games over the counter. It's worth mentioning now that even the simplest child's game can have a place in adult education if it's applied correctly.

Training games are now found in all sections of all kinds of education. It's important that the trainer realizes, however, that a game is not played just because someone else has said 'There should be a game played here'.

100 Training Games will firstly look at the academic differences between games, simulations, brain teasers, role-plays and case studies. It will also address the problem of when to use training games. The largest (and most important) section of the book is a selection of favorite training games and brain teasers. Lastly a bibliography is included for new trainers to use as a resource and for further reference.

It's worthwhile noting that trainers and facilitators these days tend to call all of these activities 'structured experiences' or 'structured exercises'. So when you hear these terms being used you will know that they are still talking about the same things. For the bulk of the information contained in this book I have referred to most games, simulations, brain teasers and role-plays as exercises. To me it's not that important which term is used as long as the trainer knows what the desired outcome is.

Most of the exercises are written as directions, rather than in the third person; however, where necessary I refer to the leader as the facilitator rather than as the trainer. In most structured exercises it is important for the leader not to be a dominant figure. Generally, if you use the term 'facilitator' that lets the group know that they aren't going to be taught by a trainer but rather find out for themselves through experience.

With the exercises contained in this handbook, I would suggest that the reader/user apply commonsense to using the enlarging facilities on their photocopier to make appropriate size overhead transparencies. This will save presentation time by reducing the amount of writing required. My policy regarding reproducing any material from this handbook is based on encouraging interprofessional networking. Therefore the material contained in this book may be freely reproduced for educational purposes or training activities. You are not required to obtain special permission for such uses. It is requested, however, that the following statement appear on all copies made:

Finally I would like to thank all of the authors, game designers and publishers who have allowed me to use their material for the benefit of new trainers.

I have attempted to acknowledge the source wherever possible. Where a source hasn't been acknowledged, either the source is unknown to me or my colleagues, or it is an original game design. As it's next to impossible to find the source of a story or a game on most occasions, I will now apologize if I have not acknowledged the source, or if it has not been acknowledged correctly.

THE ACTIVITIES

The differences between them all

Very few trainers agree on definitions for games, simulations and role-plays, case studies, and so on. The following definitions are very broad and are definitions that I have included for a new trainer to use. The more experience a trainer gains, the more they can apply their own definitions.

Even by looking at some of the examples given here, you will be able to see that it is difficult to even categorise some exercises into one grouping. Chess, for example, isn't strictly a game or a simulation, it's a combination of both. For those who are interested chess was developed in sixth-century India and was designed to simulate a contemporary battle.

Games

A game is an exercise where participants are involved in a contest with someone else (or a group of people) with a set of rules imposed. Games normally include some type of pay-off. Most training games are now aimed at having the individual trainees compete with themselves, rather than another trainee. This avoids the situation of having winners and losers.

The term 'games' includes psychomotor skills games, intellectual skills games and most games of chance. Some common types of games include darts, snakes and ladders, football, scrabble, charades and most card games. Games for individuals to play, competing with themselves, include solitaire, patience, crossword puzzles and even poker machines.

Simulations

A simulation is a mock-up of an actual or imaginary situation. Simulations are generally used to train future operators where it is impractical or too dangerous for trainees to use real-life equipment or locations. Simulations are normally designed to be as realistic as possible so that trainees can learn from their actions without the financial worries of repairing or replacing damaged equipment.

Examples of simulations include flight simulators, driving simulators, and war games.

Brain teasers

Brain teasers are in a class of their own. They aren't pure games or simulations but puzzles that either keep participants' minds busy or highlight key points. Brain teasers generally don't have any rules, but they do allow the trainer to design their own rules to suit the individual training session.

Typical brain teasers include exercises such as joining the dots and most perception exercises.

Role-plays

Role-plays are used in training to see how participants react in certain situations before and after training sessions. Role-plays are very useful for giving participants practice in dealing with other people in any given scenario. Even when the participant does it wrong, they still learn.

Case studies

Case studies are exactly what the name implies. A case (normally from the participants' workplace) is studied either by the group or by the individual. An in-depth study of a real-life or simulated scenario is undertaken to illustrate certain outcomes. When the group or the individual has the answer to the problem or situation it can be compared to what really happened and what the outcomes were.

When should they be used?

Training exercises may be used at any time during the training as long as they are relevant to the point or have been designed with a specific purpose.

The 'specific purpose' can be to keep the group occupied while waiting for stragglers, and to wake participants up after a lunch break. These purposes are okay as long as they are stated. It's not okay when they are used simply to fill in time or to make the facilitator look like a magician.

You can also use structured exercises as a means of channelling excess energy or to liven up the class. The activity can be a means of improving the learning atmosphere.

So these types of structured exercises should be selected and used on the basis of their usefulness, for reinforcing the instruction, or improving the learning environment.

Facilitator's responsibilities

Regardless of how good we are as presenters or lecturers, we shouldn't fool ourselves into thinking that our whole presentation alone is going to keep everyone's interest for the whole period. The use of games, simulations, role-plays, brain teasers, case studies and other related activities are all applications of the principles of adult learning. You, the facilitator, must ensure that the participants do not become so involved in the activity that they actually miss the learning point. Additionally you must also realise that if the participants have too high a level of enthusiasm for the exercises they may become bored with normal training. This isn't to say that we don't want high levels of enthusiasm, but we need to ensure we keep the participants interested with other methods of instruction as well.

The learning process can be sped up by the use of games, simulations, role-plays, brain teasers, case studies and other related activities. People learn better when they are enjoying themselves. So therefore we need to seriously think about creating or supplying the appropriate learning atmosphere.

You should always select the training method after you have set the learning objectives. The method should respond to the participants' needs, not the facilitator's.

When you decide to use a structured exercise it is important to practise the exercise at least once with a group of people not involved with the immediate presentation. This will help you see if the design is going to work, and in the expected way with the expected results. Like all types of training, these structured exercises must be evaluated for their worth and effectiveness. If they don't produce what is needed, scrap or modify them.

Do you have a responsibility for entertaining the group during any presentation? You have the responsibility for ensuring clarity and precision of information. You are also responsible for aligning the group and keeping them moving. Another responsibility is to keep yourself animated. (That could be considered the main entertainment value.) This is also what the participants may talk about later to their friends and colleagues. If the facilitator is in a situation where this type of feedback is required (such as an external trainer or consultant), then an assortment of training methods will be required. Games, simulations, role-plays and structured exercises will be of assistance.

It is your responsibility to pilot or test all new exercises or exercises that you haven't used in the past. Facilitators must realise that what works for some people doesn't always work for others. All training exercises will probably have different outcomes every time you use them. So be prepared.

Trainers and facilitators must debrief all of the exercises carried out during any type of training session. The purpose of debriefing is quite complicated. Without going into too much detail there are two main reasons for conducting the debriefing session.

You have an obligation to put the players or participants back together when the exercise has finished. This means that if participants have bad feelings about the exercise they should be allowed to get things off their chest while still in the training room and also while things are still fresh in their minds.

Debriefing also allows the trainer and the participants to talk about the outcomes of the exercise. Was it what everyone expected? Would you do that in the real situation? What would you have done if this had happened? It also allows the trainer a time where mistakes can be corrected.

Probably the most important point is that trainers must be completely honest and open with their participants. This includes not using hidden agendas, not misleading participants, not setting anyone up, not deceiving any of the participants and not using the participants' efforts for your own gain.

Training exercises can be lots of fun for both the

trainee and the facilitator. While people are enjoying themselves in the classroom they are generally learning better. So it's up to you to make a more enjoyable learning atmosphere.

When can these exercises be used?

Rather than fully catalogue these exercises and possibly limit their application, I have decided to use a coding system. Beside the name of the exercises on the following pages you will see one or some of the following letters and symbols. These have been placed there to give you suggested applications. *These are only guides and can be modified to suit by the individual trainer.*

Coding

 I   Icebreaker

    T   Team-building

    C   Communication

    F   Facilitator/presentation skills

    M   Mid-course energiser

 L   Learning

 P   Perception

 E   Evaluation

 S   Self-management

A full breakdown of the exercises has been included on the next few pages of this handbook. Firstly, each of the nine different categories has been given a detailed overview. The second list is an index of the hundred exercises included in this book, with full cross-referencing for each application for which they can be used.

I   Icebreaker

Almost any exercise can be used as an icebreaker. The two main purposes of using icebreakers are firstly, to allow the participants to introduce themselves to each other, and secondly, to lead into the topic matter. Participants often find that the topic matter is made clearer by the use of appropriate icebreakers.

The exercises in this grouping are non-threatening introductory contacts. They are designed to allow participants to get to know each other a little and to lower any barriers that may exist. Experienced facilitators have found that the success or failure of a program may hinge on these two points.

The more comfortable participants feel with each other, the better the learning environment. If the participants feel comfortable with each other, they are more likely to participate and to generate new ideas.

While most facilitators won't see these exercises as too threatening, some participants may. If a participant does see it as threatening, make sure they have a way out of participating. It is a wise decision to let people know at the very beginning of a program that they can pass on any exercise or activity they feel uncomfortable with.

T   Team-building

Team-building exercises are used to improve the relationship of the individuals and subgroups within a group. The term 'group' in team-building normally refers to an established work group or a group which will be working together.

When using team-building exercises you, as well as the group, should be aware that the identification of a conflict or problem between different parties or individuals may be the only outcome of some team-building exercises. However, a conflict or problem is much easier to solve or deal with after it has been identified. A team-building exercise should allow the participants to let their hair down while they get to know each other.

It is very important that you thoroughly debrief team-building exercises to ensure that there isn't any built up hostility, anger or frustration. Don't let the group break until this has been rectified.

C Communication

Exercises used for communication are designed to let the participants find out where certain communication skills may be improved. You, as facilitator, have to be very aware of the exact purpose of some communication exercises as it is sometimes very difficult to sit back and say nothing while things start to go wrong for the participant.

You also need to be aware that you may be looked at by some participants as a role-model. While conducting a program on communication skills you must ensure that what you give out is correct. As feedback is a very important part of communication skills it must be used in all communication exercises. Feedback should be specific and aimed at observed behaviours that the individual has some control over.

F Facilitator/presentation skills

Facilitation skills are aimed at people who may need to develop or improve their up-front, or presentation, ability. The exercises in this category are designed to get the participants thinking about particular aspects of their own presentation and facilitation skills.

While using any exercises to improve presentation skills you should take full advantage of the opportunity by using the individuals in the group wherever possible. This may mean getting some of them to run the exercises. It is important that the facilitator ensures the individuals are observed and debriefed by the rest of the group. By this simple observation group members are able to see things that may or may not work for them. The more styles of presentation they see, the better.

Some of these exercises can be seen as very threatening to a few group members, so make sure you are prepared to offer support and assistance.

M Mid-course energiser

Mid-course energisers can be used at any time you observe the group losing interest or falling asleep. Mid-course energisers are very similar in design to icebreakers, but they sometimes make the assumption that the group knows each other already. For this reason some of the exercises may appear a little threatening to some members of a group. If someone does not want to participate, let them sit back or act in an observer's role. You will normally find that they will join in as soon as they see how much fun the others are having.

These exercises are used to wake participants up, to get the blood moving, to keep participants from falling asleep after a lunch break, to simply get people back on line or to think about a new approach to a problem.

Experienced facilitators can also use these energisers to reduce tensions that may have built up with individuals or the group.

L Learning

These exercises are designed to let the participants see where their learning styles or attitudes need improvement. They tend to be more experiential in their application. That is, the participants are normally required to do something and come up with some kind of result or answer. After that phase of the exercise the facilitator can normally draw out from the group better ways of doing the same thing with better results.

You must ensure that the whole exercise is totally debriefed and that every participant can see what the final results or methods should be. You should be aware that there are many different learning styles. Don't make the assumption that everyone in the group will learn the same way. Make certain you get plenty of feedback to check participant understanding.

P Perception

The perception exercises are generally fun for everyone to use. They are designed to see how participants perceive different situations or objects. The end result with most perception exercises is that participants are made aware of their need to use lateral thinking, to look at things in different ways, and to try to break down any preconceived stereotypes that they may be using.

As these exercise are fun to use, it is not uncommon to see them being used as icebreakers or mid-course energisers.

Some of the individuals in the group may have difficulty with perception exercises. If they do have difficulties, try to get the rest of the group to explain the different perceptions to them.

E Evaluation

Most of the evaluation exercises are for participants to evaluate either themselves or the program. An important part of the evaluation process needs to be pointed out to the participants at the beginning of the exercise. This point is that any evaluation must be considered as constructive, not destructive. Things can be improved or rectified much more easily by using constructive evaluation. Destructive evaluation does nothing but leave ill-feelings with some members.

If any of these exercises are used for the purpose of program evaluation, it is a good idea to make sure the participants are told of the results, either verbally or in writing.

S Self-management

Exercises in the category of self-management allow the participants to find where they can improve their own self-management techniques. These techniques are the same as time-management techniques, but with a different name. Here we look at improving the participants' organisational skills.

Participants get a lot of information and new ideas from other members within the group, so make sure that the whole group finds out what principles each participant used in these exercises.

Games Codes Grid

No.	Name	Page	Category									
1.	Too Many Solutions?	18	TCF		●	●	●					
2.	Relay	19	ITCM	●	●	●		●				
3.	Human Machines	20	ITM	●	●			●				
4.	Garage Sale	21	I	●								
5.	Clear the Deck	22	I	●								
6.	New Ideas	24	CFM			●	●	●				
7.	I Am …	25	I	●								
8.	Telling Lies	27	IMP	●				●		●		
9.	AAA of Stress Management	28	TS		●							●
10.	Introductions	30	I	●								
11.	Signatures	32	IF	●			●					
12.	Join the Dots	33	IMP	●				●		●		
13.	Brain Teasers	38	ICMP	●		●		●		●		
14.	Scavenger Hunt	40	ITCM	●	●	●		●				
15.	Brainstorm Destruction	42	CF			●	●					
16.	Action Plans	43	S									●
17.	Stretch Monitor	45	IFM	●			●	●				
18.	Tied in Knots	46	ITM	●	●			●				
19.	Common Words	47	ICML	●		●		●	●			
20.	What's Your Name?	49	ICL	●		●			●			
21.	Beans	50	MP					●		●		
22.	Pass It On	52	CFML			●	●	●	●			
23.	Building Blocks	54	C			●						
24.	Put Your Jacket On	55	ICF	●		●	●					
25.	Light Your Cigarette	56	CFMP			●	●	●		●		
26.	Stepping In	57	ITM	●	●			●				
27.	Manipulation	58	ICFMP	●		●	●	●		●		
28.	What Do People Want?	59	ICP	●		●				●		
29.	Capital Punishment	61	IM	●				●				
30.	The Word Game	63	ICM	●		●		●				
31.	Spelling Bee	65	CML			●		●	●			
32.	Another Spelling Bee	67	CML			●		●	●			
33.	Team Task No. 1	69	TMP		●			●		●		
34.	Team Task No. 2	71	TMP		●			●		●		
35.	3-Minute Test	73	ICM	●		●		●				
36.	Pass the Microphone	75	CF			●	●					
37.	The Watch Face	76	IP	●						●		
38.	Relaxation	77	S									●
39.	Note to Me	78	LES						●		●	●
40.	The Numbers Game	79	IMLES	●				●	●		●	●
41.	Puppets	81	M					●				
42.	No Laughing	82	IM	●				●				
43.	Shuffling Papers	83	ITM	●	●			●				
44.	Cleaning Up	84	TM		●			●				
45.	What Do You See?	85	CMP			●		●		●		
46.	Smile	87	I	●								
47.	Stress Budget	89	IMPS	●				●		●		●
48.	Negotiation	90	ICMLS	●		●		●	●			●
49.	Our Greatest Fears	91	IF	●			●					
50.	Marooned	93	IM	●				●				

14

Games Codes Grid

No. Name	Page	Category	✍	🤝	〰	👉	🏋	🎓	👁	⚖	📄
51. Signs	94	IM	●				●				
52. Balloon Ball	96	ITM	●	●			●				
53. Tortoise, Hare or Thoroughbred	97	IMS	●				●				
54. Where Are We Now?	99	ITCFP	●	●	●	●			●		
55. Overcoming Fear	100	FS				●					
56. Memory Test	102	ICMLPS	●		●		●	●	●		
57. Say What?	104	IC	●		●						
58. Room 703	105	ITCM	●	●	●		●				
59. List of Names	107	TCPS		●	●				●		
60. Folding Paper	108	ICFPE	●		●	●			●	●	
61. Learning by Linking	109	ICMLS	●		●		●	●			
62. What Is It?	112	ICFMP	●		●	●	●		●		
63. Circuit Overload	114	S			●						
64. Tangrams	116	ITCMP	●	●	●		●		●		
65. In-Tray	119	CS			●						
66. tebahplA ehT	120	ICFMLS	●		●	●	●	●			
67. How's Your Memory?	122	ITCMPS	●	●	●		●		●		
68. Tennis Balls	124	IM	●				●				
69. Having Fun	126	S									
70. My Worries	128	IS	●								
71. Moon Explorer Problem	130	TCMP		●	●		●		●		
72. Fall-out Shelter	132	TCMP		●	●		●		●		
73. A Case of Labelling	134	IP	●						●		
74. Faces	135	I	●								
75. Follow-up to Murphy's Law	137	IM	●				●				
76. Them and Us	139	TCP		●	●				●		
77. The Brainstorm	141	CMLS			●		●	●			
78. Clasp Your Hands	142	ICS	●		●						
79. Fold Your Arms	143	ICS	●		●						
80. Clowns	144	ITCES	●	●						●	
81. What's My Object?	146	ICMPS	●		●		●		●		
82. Come Back	147	IFS	●			●					
83. Post-it	148	FE				●				●	
84. 15 Pieces	149	TC		●	●						
85. Housie	151	I	●								
86. Participant Bingo	152	I	●								
87. Pick a Shape	154	IM	●				●				
88. 2-Minute Talk	156	CFS		●		●					●
89. Where Did It Go?	157	IES	●							●	
90. Post Me a Note	159	ITCES	●	●	●					●	
91. Spider's Web	160	TE		●						●	
92. Personally	161	E								●	
93. The Application	162	PES							●	●	
94. Clap	163	M					●				
95. Time Line	164	CS			●						
96. Orientation Quiz	165	I	●								
97. People Scavenger	166	I	●								
98. Co-operation	168	ITCMP	●	●	●		●		●		
99. Paper Planes	169	TCMS		●	●		●				
100. Agenda	171	ITC	●	●	●						

THE
GAMES

1. Too Many Solutions?

Overview
This game looks at the use of brainstorming with a group of participants working on a given problem.

Goals
1. To develop skills in problem-solving.
2. To generate as many ideas as possible from a group using brainstorming techniques.
3. To introduce and apply synergy.

Time required
30-60 minutes (depending on the type of problem given).

Size of group
Unlimited, but needs to be broken into subgroups of 5–7 participants.

Material required
Flipchart paper and felt markers for each subgroup.

Procedure
1. Break the group into teams of 5–7 participants.
2. Give the teams a problem to solve. The problem can either be work based or imaginary. For example, how can we get more customers in the store? Or, how do we sell ice to the Eskimos?
3. *Rules:*
   Each team is to elect a scribe/spokesperson. The scribe is to elicit as many ideas as possible from the other team members in a period of 10–15 minutes. No discussion of suggestions is to take place until the 10–15 minute period is up.

The scribes are requested to encourage ridiculous ideas from their team members.

When the 10–15 minute period is up, each team is then to evaluate each of the ideas generated by it. It is to decide on the best three ideas. On reaching agreement each spokesperson is to present the team findings to the whole group.

Once each team has presented its findings, the whole group is then to decide on the single best idea presented.

Discussion points
1. Which team had the greatest number of ideas? Why?
2. Was anyone surprised at the number of ideas generated?
3. Did the ridiculous ideas lead to more productive ideas?
4. Who had trouble with the concept of not discussing each idea as it was generated?
5. Which team members were encouraging other team members for more ideas?

Variations
1. If the group has a common problem, use it for the exercise.
2. Each team can be given a different problem to work on.

Trainer's notes

Overview
Participants pass cards as quickly as possible in relay style. This is used as an icebreaking activity.

Goals
1. To develop team-building.
2. To get the group 'warmed up'.
3. To open communication within each team.
4. To introduce and apply synergy.

Time required
10–15 minutes (depending on group size).

Size of group
Unlimited, but needs to be broken into subgroups of 5–7 participants.

Material required
A pack of playing cards for each group.

Procedure
1. Break the group into subgroups of 5–7 participants.
2. Members of each subgroup position their chairs in a line side by side. It's best if the subgroups can all see each other (this sets up competition).
3. Tell the subgroups to be seated and that this is a competitive game.
4. *Rules:*
   The players at one end of each line must take one card at a time off their pile of cards which is located on the floor beside their chair. When they have picked the card up they must pass it to the closest hand of the team member sitting next to them. The second team member then places the card in the other hand and then passes it on to the third team member's closest hand, and so on. When the final team member receives a card they must place it on a pile beside their chair.

   If a team member drops a card the rest of the team must wait until the card has been picked up again before continuing. Each team member must not hold more than one card at a time.

   All 52 cards must be used and are to be counted at the end of the game.

   Teams will have 5 minutes to plan their strategies before the starting time.
5. The team that completes the exercise first is declared the winner.

Discussion points
1. How did the winning team win?
2. Who led the 5-minute planning session? Why?
3. Who dropped cards? Why? (Due to stress?)
4. Was the planning stage of any value to the groups? Why?
5. Can this exercise be related to the workplace?

Variation
1. Blindfolds may be used by all or some of the team members.
2. Coins may be substituted instead of playing cards.
3. The cards may be required to be returned back down the line.

Source
Adapted from 'Card Relay', Sue Forbess-Greene, *The Encyclopedia of Icebreakers*, University Associates, California, 1983.

Trainer's notes

3. Human Machines

Overview
In this exercise the participants are to form teams and build a human machine.

Goals
1. To liven the group up after lunch.
2. To develop team-building.

Time required
10–15 minutes.

Size of group
Unlimited, but broken into teams. Ideally teams should be 8–12 participants.

Material required
None.

Procedure
1. Break the group into teams.
2. Give the teams 5 minutes to design a human machine where the members are all components of the machine. All of the human components rely on each other for movement, that is, one action leads to another.
3. When the planning time has ended each team is to demonstrate its 'human machine'.
4. The whole group is to select the best design.

Discussion points
1. Did everyone feel comfortable with the exercise?
2. Has everyone's lunch now settled?

Variations
1. After each team has demonstrated its design, all of the 'human machines' may be joined together.
2. The design period may be carried out non-verbally.
3. The facilitator may have prepared slips of paper with machine titles that each team has to work to. These machines could include a sausage making machine, a large clock, a fire engine, a bicycle, a calculator, a paddle-steamer, a typewriter, a coffee percolator, a concrete mixer, etc.

Trainer's notes

4. Garage Sale

Overview

Participants select an object from a table and tell the group why they chose it.

Goal

1. To get to know each other.

Time required

10 minutes plus 1–2 minutes for every participant.

Size of group

Up to 16. Becomes too time-consuming with larger groups.

Material required

A table with a selection of goods that may be seen at a garage sale or in a 'junk' drawer or cupboard. The number of items needs to be more than the number of participants. A large sheet of paper or a large cloth is needed to cover all of the items before the exercise commences.

Procedure

1. Place all the articles on a table and cover them with a cloth before the group comes into the room.
2. Tell the participants that when the cloth is removed they are to come up and select an item from the table that for some reason appeals to them.
3. After everyone has selected an item, they are to introduce themselves to the group and state why that particular item appealed to them.

Discussion points

1. Did anyone see that some of the items selected suited the person who chose it?
2. Did anyone see an item that appeared to match other participants? Why?

Variation

1. Get a participant to introduce him/herself to the group. Then have another member select an item off the table that they feel suits the person just introduced. Have them explain why they see an association. Repeat for everyone in the group.

Trainer's notes

Overview
This script is designed to get participants to leave any worries they have outside the training room.

Goals
1. To get participants ready for learning.
2. To introduce a simple stress relieving exercise.

Time required
10–15 minutes.

Size of group
Unlimited.

Material required
A copy of the 'Clear the Deck Guided Fantasy Script'.

Procedure
1. Tell participants to find a comfortable position for this exercise and then close their eyes.
2. Ask the members of the group to take a few deep breaths and then read the script slowly to them.

Discussion points
1. Does anyone want to describe their box to the group?
2. Did the exercise work? Why?
3. Can this be applied to the workplace or at home?
4. Is anyone surprised that they have the power to stop themselves from worrying with a simple exercise?

Variations
1. At the conclusion of the exercise have everyone draw their 'box' and show it to another participant.
2. Have the script prerecorded on a cassette with background music.

Source
Adapted from 'Clear the Deck', Nancy Loving Tubesing and Donald A. Tubesing, *Structured Exercises in Stress Management*, Volume 1, Whole Person Press, Duluth MN, 1983.

Trainer's notes

Clear the deck guided fantasy script (to be read slowly)

I'd like you to take a few minutes to focus on the various concerns, preoccupations and worries that you've brought here with you today.

There may be any number of things on your mind: whether you remembered to turn off the electric jug this morning before you left home, (pause) perhaps an unfinished conversation you were having with someone, (pause) maybe you're thinking about the things that you need to do when you get home this afternoon, (pause) or the things that have to be done at the office tomorrow.

Take a moment to really focus on what these concerns are for you right now, (pause) and develop a mental list.

These concerns that you have listed are making claims on your energy. These concerns are stopping you from being fully present here today.

Probably there is nothing that you can do during the next (_____ hours/minutes) about these concerns, except to worry, (pause) and that will distract you from all that you can be learning here, (pause) so let's put those worries away for a while.

I'd like you to create in your mind a box, (pause) with a lid on it, (pause) and a lock and a key. (pause) The box can be any size and shape that you want it to be, (pause) but it needs to be large enough and strong enough to hold all the concerns that you've identified. (pause) So take a moment to visualise this box as clearly as you can. (pause) The box is now in front of you with the lid open.

Now I'd like you to put each of your concerns in the box, one by one, (pause) make sure that they all go in. (pause) As you are doing this say to yourself, 'There is nothing I can do about this for now, (pause) and so I'm going to put these concerns away in this safe, secure box while I'm here, (pause) and I know I can come back later and reclaim all of my concerns'.

Now when you've put all of your preoccupations and concerns in the box, I'd like you to close the lid and lock it with your key. (pause) Now I'd like you to put the key in your pocket or someplace else for safekeeping, (pause) and remember that at the end of this program, you can unlock your box and pick up where you left off.

And when you're ready, I'd like you to slowly open your eyes and come back here.

6. New Ideas

Overview
Participants are given a problem to think about and solve. The ideas are rated by other group members.

Goals
1. To encourage group participation.
2. To get the participants thinking and talking about common problems.

Time required
5 minutes plus 2–5 minutes for each participant.

Size of group
Unlimited, but subgroups would need to be formed if there are more than about 20 participants.

Material required
3 sets of scoring cards (cards with numbers 1–10 on them).

Procedure
1. At the conclusion of the first day, give participants a problem to think about and ask them to come up with a solution for the next morning. The problem should be relevant to all of the participants. It works best if the topic area is part of the second day's presentation.
2. At the beginning of the second day select 3 judges from the group and give each a set of scoring cards. Seat them at the front of the room.
3. Participants are then to give their solutions to the problem one at a time. As each participant gives a solution the judges show the card they have selected as a score for that idea, 10 being the highest award by each judge.
4. After all participants have given their solutions, check the scores and announce the winner.

Discussion points
1. Who gained a new solution that they hadn't considered?
2. When people heard other participants' solutions, did they think of other possible solutions or ways to improve their ideas?

Variation
1. Teams may be formed and given different problems to solve. When each team presents its solution, all other teams then score the solution proposed.

Source
Adapted from 'Swap Shop', John W. Newstrom and Edward E. Scannell, *Games Trainers Play*, McGraw-Hill, Inc., New York, 1980.

Trainer's notes

Overview

Participants write down items about themselves for other group members to see. This icebreaker can be used at the beginning of a course where participants do not know each other.

Goals

1. To encourage group participation.
2. To get to know each other.

Time required

30–40 minutes.

Size of group

Unlimited.

Material required

A sheet of paper for each participant with 'I Am ...' written on the top of it. A pen for each participant and tape or pins to attach the sheet to the front of each participant's shirt or blouse.

Procedure

1. Hand out an 'I Am ...' sheet and a pen to each participant.
2. Tell participants they have 10 minutes to write 10 responses to the question.
3. When the preparation time has finished tell the participants to attach their sheet to the front of their shirt or blouse and then walk around the room reading other participants' sheets. This phase is carried out in silence.
4. After 10 minutes the participants are told to talk to the people whose sheets appeared to be interesting or ask any questions they may have thought of while reading the sheets.

Discussion points

1. Did anyone find people with similar responses to theirs?
2. Did people feel threatened writing the information down, knowing that others were going to see it?

Variations

1. Other phrases such as 'I want to be ...', '10 things I like about myself are ...' may be used.
2. Step 3 may be deleted.

Source

Adapted from 'Who am I?: A Getting Acquainted Activity', J. William Pfeiffer and John E. Jones, *A Handbook of Structured Experiences for Human Relations Training*, Volume 1, University Associates, California, 1975.

Trainer's notes

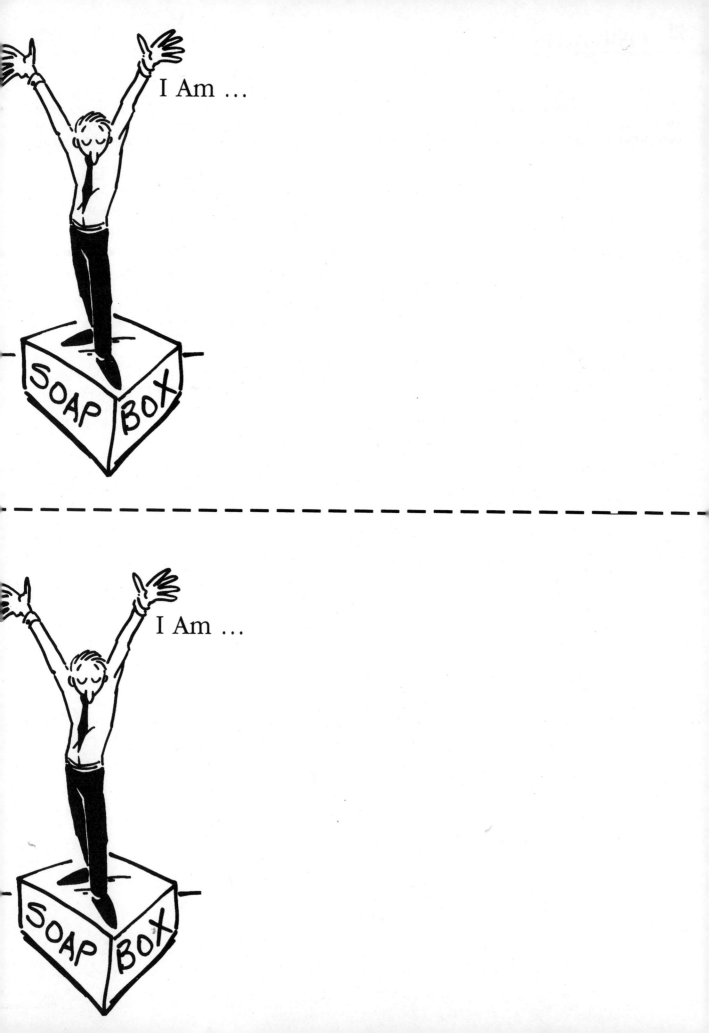

I Am ...

SOAP BOX

I Am ...

SOAP BOX

8. Telling Lies

Overview
This exercise allows participants to get to know each other a little better.

Goals
1. To introduce the participants to each other.
2. To allow participants to get to know each other.
3. To liven people up after a break.

Time required
10–30 minutes, depending on group size.

Size of group
Unlimited.

Material required
A prize.

Procedure
1. Inform the group members that they are going to introduce themselves, one at a time, to the rest of the group. This introduction is to include things such as their name, position, interests, hobbies, and so on. Tell them that one of the things they say about themselves is to be a lie.
2. The participants are now allowed to introduce themselves after the facilitator starts. After each introduction the group has to decide which piece of information is the lie.
3. After everyone has introduced themselves and their lie, ask the group to vote on the best or most imaginative lie. Give the person who wins a small prize.

Discussion points
1. Which were the best lies? Why?
2. Is it easier to pick when some people lie?
3. Why are some people more convincing?

Variation
1. The guesses as to participant lies can be left to the end of the introductions, or until the end of the course. This will mean however that all participants will need to take notes.

Trainer's notes

9. AAA of Stress Management

Overview
This exercise looks at one technique of stress management.

Goals
1. To find a method of stress management.
2. To apply that technique to a stressful situation.

Time required
30 minutes.

Size of group
Unlimited.

Material required
2 'AAA Stress Management Forms' and a pen for each participant.

Procedure
1. Ask for some examples of stress-management techniques. Discuss these briefly.
2. Tell the group of the 3 A's used in stress management. These are Alter, Avoid and Accept. Discuss these techniques with the group. (The facilitator bases this information on the 'AAA Stress Management Form'.)
3. Hand out the 'AAA Stress Management Form'.
4. Read out the following scenario to the group: 'You have just been transferred to a new position in a new part of your organisation. Your new supervisor doesn't appear to like you very much. They seem to be giving you all the "dirty work" and then avoiding you. The only feedback you are getting from them is when things aren't done correctly. The supervisor obviously thinks that you can't do the job properly.'
5. Get all of the participants to use the 'AAA Stress Management Form' for this scenario.

6. After all participants have completed the form they are to talk in pairs and tell each other why they recommended what they did as the best option.
7. After this discussion period get the best 2 or 3 ideas from the group.
8. Now give each participant 10 minutes to think of a stressful situation they presently have at home. They are then to use the 'AAA Stress Management Form' to see if they can come up with an option for themselves.
9. At the end of this session ask them to put the form in their pocket or bag for reference when they get home. When there they should apply their best option.
10. Ask participants at the next session if their solution worked or not. If possible, get at least 2 participants to tell the group how they reduced their stress using their best option.

Discussion points
1. Does anyone in the group presently use a similar technique? Does it work for them?
2. Can different people have different best options for the same stressful situation? Why?

Variations
1. The facilitator should write a scenario that is relevant to the group's needs.
2. The group may be broken into smaller groups and given different scenarios.

Source
Adapted from 'AAAbc's of Stress Management', Nancy Loving Tubesing and Donald A. Tubesing, *Structured Exercises in Stress Management*, Volume 1, Whole Person Press, Duluth MN, 1983.

Trainer's notes

AAA Stress Management Form

Scenario:

Alter: (How could you remove the source of stress?)

Avoid: (How could you get away from or avoid the source of stress?)

Accept: (How could you live with the stress?)

Build up resistance by …

Change self and/or perceptions by …

Best option is:

Overview

This exercise allows participants to get to know each other a little better. It has been designed for use at the beginning of a program but may also be used at any stage during the program.

Goal

1. To get to know each other.

Time required

15–20 minutes.

Size of group

Unlimited.

Material required

A copy of the 'Introduction Sheet' and a pen for each participant. Pins or tape will also be required to attach the sheet to the front of each participant's shirt or blouse.

Procedure

1. Give each participant an 'Introduction Sheet'.
2. Tell participants to write their name at the top and then fill in the next 6 pieces of information.
3. When all participants have completed their sheets, they should be pinned or stuck on the front of their shirt or blouse.
4. Then tell participants to pair up with someone and read their 'Introduction Sheet'. Participants talk for 2 minutes and then change partners. This is repeated as many times as you feel necessary.

Discussion points

1. Did anyone find someone else with a similar 'Introduction Sheet'?
2. Who had the most unusual response in each area?
3. Did everyone meet someone new?

Variations

1. You could select other areas of information to be given.
2. After the sheets have been completed you could decide to include a non-verbal phase where the participants just walk around reading other participants' 'Introduction Sheets'. This would be followed by the 2-minute meeting periods.

Trainer's notes

Introduction Sheet

Name:

My favourite   sport is:
                    animal is:
                    country is:
                    person is:
                    food is:
                    hobby is:

- -

Introduction Sheet

Name:

My favourite   sport is:
                    animal is:
                    country is:
                    person is:
                    food is:
                    hobby is:

- -

Introduction Sheet

Name:

My favourite   sport is:
                    animal is:
                    country is:
                    person is:
                    food is:
                    hobby is:

- -

Introduction Sheet

Name:

My favourite   sport is:
                    animal is:
                    country is:
                    person is:
                    food is:
                    hobby is:

11. Signatures

Overviews
This is a simple exercise to be used as an icebreaker.

Goal
1. To allow participants to introduce themselves to the group.

Time required
10–20 minutes depending on group size.

Size of group
Unlimited.

Material required
A flipchart or whiteboard.

Procedure
1. Tell the group members that they are going to introduce themselves individually to the group.
2. The participants go up to the whiteboard or flipchart one at a time and sign their names. Then they introduce themselves, and hand on the marker to another participant. This is repeated until everyone has been introduced to the group.

Discussion points
1. How did people feel standing up the front introducing themselves?
2. How do people control nerves in front of a group?

Variations
1. You, as facilitator, may start by signing your name and making the first introduction.
2. The order can be preselected, that is, going around the room.
3. If an electronic whiteboard is used for this exercise, you can make a copy of the board after everyone has signed their name. This can then be reproduced and given to all of the participants as a memento of the program.

Trainer's notes

Overview

This simple but effective exercise gets participants into the idea of thinking outside of our 'self-limiting boxes'. It may also be used to fill in time at the beginning of the day while waiting for latecomers to arrive.

Goal

1. To allow participants to see that the answers to some problems lie outside their normal boundary of thinking.

Time required

10–15 minutes.

Size of group

Unlimited.

Material required

3 sheets of paper and a pen for each participant. A whiteboard or flipchart to draw the dots on, or a prepared overhead transparency.

Procedure

1. Tell the participants that ours is a traditional way of thinking for solving problems. Hand out the paper and pens.
2. Give the participants the 9-dot problem. Tell them that they have 2 minutes to join the dots with 4 consecutive straight lines and that they are not allowed to lift their pen off the paper or repeat a line.
3. After the 2-minute period show the participants the

way that it's done. Reinforce the idea that they have to think beyond the 'self-limiting boxes' that we sometimes place on our thinking.

4. Next give them the 12-dot problem. They must join the 12 dots with 5 consecutive straight lines. Again they are not allowed to lift their pen off the paper or repeat a line.
5. For the participants who haven't arrived at the correct solution, show them the answer and again reinforce the idea of thinking outside self-imposed boundaries.
6. Finally give them the 16-dot problem. They must join the 16 dots with 6 consecutive straight lines. They are still not allowed to lift their pen off the paper or repeat a line.
7. Show the solution to all of the participants who are struggling to find an answer. Again reinforce that they must increase their thinking limits.
8. Optional: Before concluding this exercise let the group know that there is a second solution to the joining of the 9 dots. Let them have overnight to find the second solution.

Discussion points

1. Was anyone able to solve all 3 problems?
2. Can everyone see now that we do impose boundaries on our thinking?
3. Can this application be used in the workplace?

Variations

1. The 3 exercises can be used at different times during the course.
2. Only 1 or 2 of the problems may be used.

Trainer's notes

Solution

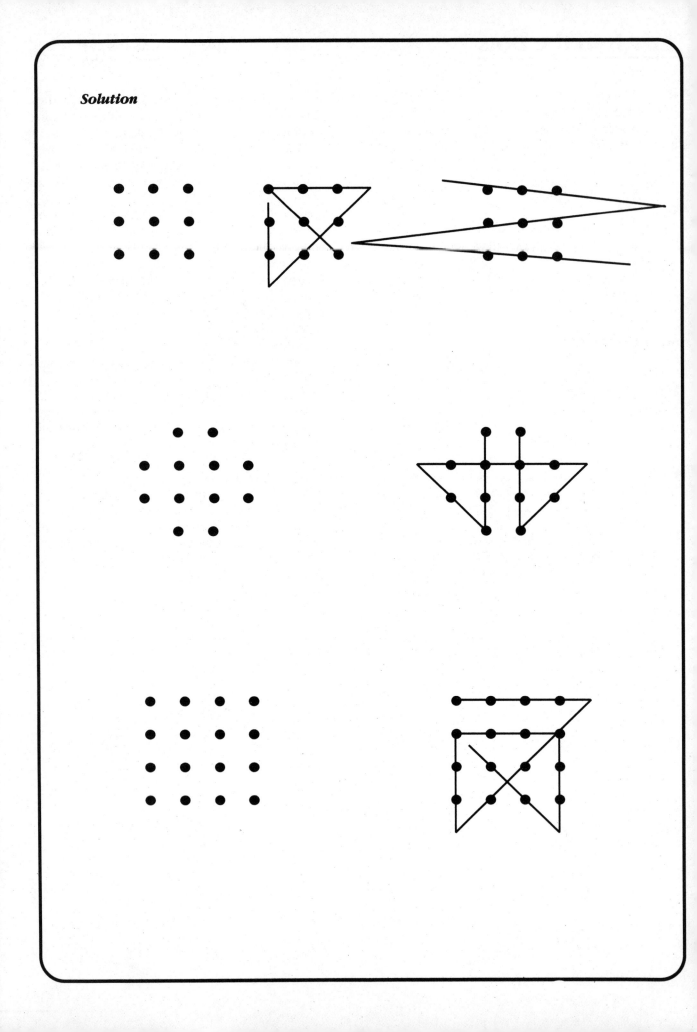

Join the Dots

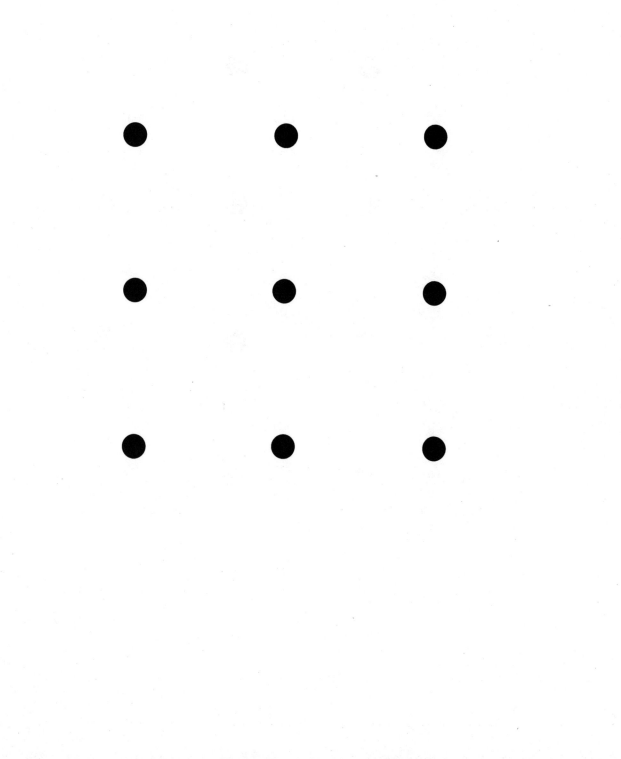

Join the Dots

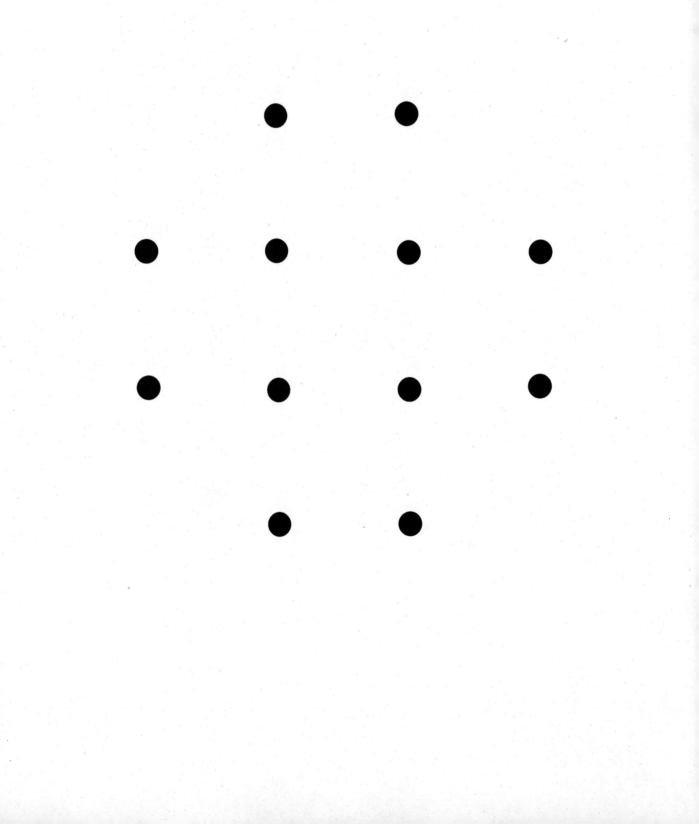

Join the Dots

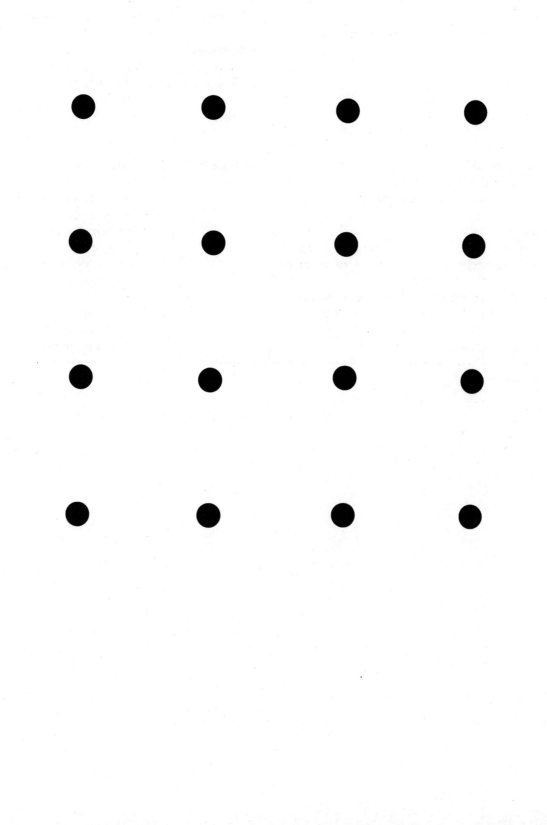

13. Brain Teasers

Overview

This mixed bag of brain teasers can be used at any time during training to liven the group up or simply to fill in time while waiting for latecomers to arrive.

Goals

1. To liven the group up after a break.
2. To see the basic idea of one of the brainstorming principles.
3. To keep the mind occupied while waiting.

Time required

5–10 minutes.

Size of group

Unlimited.

Material required

A prepared handout, overhead transparency or flipchart with the brain teasers appearing.

Procedure

1. Let the participants know that you are going to show them a series of brain teasers for them to solve.
2. Display the brain teasers and get the participants to call out what they believe they indicate. You should process this exercise similar to a brainstorming session.

3. When the correct response is given, move straight on to the next problem.

Discussion points

1. Who got most of them right?
2. Point out that we all tend to see differently.
3. You may lead into techniques for brainstorming before moving on to the main session.

Variations

1. Give prizes for correct responses.
2. Break the group into teams of 5–7 participants and have them compete to see which team can solve all of the brain teasers first.

Solutions

1. Mixed feelings
2. Horseback riding
3. Up in smoke
4. The price is right
5. Mid-term exam
6. Multiple listing
7. Almost forgotten
8. Stepping out of line
9. Feet first
10. Repeat after me
11. Bee in a bonnet
12. Out-going person

Trainer's notes

Brain Teasers

1.	2.	3.	4.
G E L E N S F	ESROH RIDING	S M O K E	LEFT PRICE
5.	6.	7.	8.
TEEXAMRM	LISTING LISTING LISTING LISTING	FORGOTTE	T P G S P N E I
9.	10.	11.	12.
1. FEET 2. HANDS 3. FACE	ME/REPEAT	BONBNET	PERSON

14. Scavenger Hunt

ITCM

Overview
This exercise may be used at any stage of training to liven the group up again.

Goals
1. To liven the group up.
2. To see how resourceful team members are.

Time required
10–15 minutes.

Size of group
Unlimited, but there must be enough materials for all participants to scavenge.

Material required
A printed list of items for each group to find and a prize (such as a bag of lollies) for the winning team.

Procedure
1. Divide the group into teams of 5–7 people.
2. Tell the participants that they are all going to be involved in a scavenger hunt. A prize will be awarded to the winning team.
3. Give the scavenger hunt list to the teams. Tell them that they are to use their own resources to get all of the items.
4. Stop the exercise when the first team collects all of the items required. The group then reassembles for the award presentation.

Discussion points
1. How close were the other teams to finishing?
2. How do you feel about the winning team?
3. Did any one person in your team appear to be more resourceful or cunning than anyone else?
4. Did anyone in your team take charge? Who? Why?

Suggested items for a scavenger hunt
1. A ladies' hairbrush
2. A paperclip
3. A copy of today's newspaper
4. A handful of dirt
5. A railway ticket
6. Number of entrances to the building
7. Number of people working on this floor
8. A cold cup of coffee
9. A street directory
10. A list of the team members' names (in full)

Note: The facilitator should tailor the list to suit each group and the surroundings. Harder-to-find items can also be included if time allows.

Variation
1. Impose a time limit and make the team with the most items the winner.

Trainer's notes

Scavenger Hunt

Your team is required to collect the following items.
The time limits and point system will be explained by the leader.

Overview

In this exercise participants are to list all the phrases they can think of that will destroy a brainstorming session.

Goals

1. To make participants aware of phrases that are banned from brainstorming sessions.
2. To start applying brainstorming techniques.
3. To allow one of the group members to experience the facilitator's role.

Time required

15–20 minutes.

Size of group

Unlimited.

Material required

A whiteboard or flipchart and markers.

Procedure

1. Tell the group the rules for brainstorming. Make certain that things such as 'no judgment', 'all to participate' and 'quantity rather than quality' are reinforced as important principles of brainstorming.
2. Tell the group members that, using these techniques, they are to elect their own facilitator to lead a session.
3. Tell the elected participant to elicit as many 'blocking' brainstorming phrases as possible from the group. Remind them that there is to be no judgment or criticism allowed at all within the group.
4. Let the group members brainstorm for 10 minutes (or sooner if they run out of ideas). You may participate as a group member to keep the ideas moving and to suggest any common phrases that they may overlook.
5. Discuss the phrases that they have generated.

Discussion points

1. Discuss all of the phrases generated.
2. How did they feel not being allowed to comment on ideas given during the exercise?
3. Do they consider that this exercise was a 'model' brainstorming session? Why? Why not?

Variations

1. At the conclusion of the exercise you could copy the group's list for distribution to the members.
2. You could give the elected facilitator the list of 'Common Brainstorming Blocking Phrases' and tell that person he/she is responsible for eliciting most of these ideas from the group while still maintaining a facilitator's role.

Common brainstorming blocking phrases

The group should generate these phrases. Ensure that the group generates most of these ideas among themselves. A little prompting at times may be required.

1. That's ridiculous.
2. We don't have the time.
3. We did all right without it before.
4. Let's form a committee.
5. Why change it when it's still working okay?
6. We've never done that before.
7. We're not ready for that.
8. That's their problem, not ours.
9. Let's get back to reality.
10. Senior management won't agree to that.
11. That's not practical.
12. That will cost too much.
13. We've tried that before.
14. Has anyone else tried it before?
15. It's not in the budget.
16. You can't teach an old dog new tricks.
17. What will the union say?
18. That's not included in our responsibility.
19. Pull the other one, it laughs.
20. You should have passed on that one.

Trainer's notes

Overview

Action plans will be given to the participants to note down ideas or tasks that they want to implement back at the office or at home.

Goals

1. To make participants aware of action plans.
2. To give participants a method of taking back important ideas or tasks.

Time required

5 minutes.

Size of group

Unlimited.

Material required

A copy of the 'Action Plan' sheet for each participant.

Procedure

1. Advise the group of the importance of using ideas as soon as possible back in the 'real world'. If these ideas aren't used within 24 hours they probably will never be used.
2. Give participants a copy of the 'Action Plan' sheet and tell them that it is for their personal use during the training program.
3. Advise participants to write down any idea or task from the training session that they feel is important to them. Also tell participants that it is their responsibility to look at their 'Action Plans' when they get back to their workplace the next morning. Then anything they have noted down on their 'Action Plan' should be implemented.

Discussion points

1. How many good ideas have they heard and then forgotten?
2. Isn't it easier for people to find all of their important notes on one piece of paper rather than search through reams of paper trying to find them?

Variations

1. At the end of each training session participants could be asked to share their 'Action Plan' with the person sitting next to them.
2. The facilitator could take copies of the participants' 'Action Plan' to follow up with the individuals at a later date.

Trainer's notes

Action Plan

If you hear any good ideas or ways of performing a task a better way, this is the spot for you to write them down. It has been found that if new ideas aren't used within 24 hours, they are generally forgotten. When you get back to work put this sheet in a prominent place and make sure that you try all of the things that you have made note of.

1. _____

2. _____

3. _____

4. _____

5. _____

6. _____

7. _____

8. _____

9. _____

10. _____

11. _____

12. _____

13. _____

14. _____

15. _____

17. Stretch Monitor

Overview
This exercise should be included in the introduction of a program. It allows the participants to have an input to the pace of the program.

Goals
1. To get the group 'warmed up'.
2. To allow the participants to have their say about the pace of the program or to allow them to set breaks.

Time required
None.

Size of group
Unlimited.

Material required
None.

Procedure
1. During the initial introductions tell the group that they will be responsible for themselves not falling asleep during the program.
2. Ask for 2 or 3 volunteers to take this responsibility.
3. Tell the volunteers that they are 'stretch monitors' and that if they feel like standing up or having a stretch during the program they are to do so. Tell the other participants that they must do the same as the stretch monitors.
4. Also tell the group that you, as facilitator, don't have the power to override the stretch monitors and that you have to remain silent while the group performs its exercises.

Note: You should prompt one of the volunteers to stretch shortly into the session so that everyone can see what happens.

Discussion point
1. Can anyone suggest other types of exercises?

Variations
1. With small groups only 1 or 2 monitors are required.
2. You can make all of the participants 'stretch monitors'.

Trainer's notes

18. Tied in Knots

Overview

This is an exercise/icebreaker that energises the group while building team spirit.

Goals

1. To liven up the participants after lunch.
2. To get participants moving and laughing.
3. To increase team spirit through simple problem-solving.

Time required

10–15 minutes.

Size of group

Unlimited if time permits. Normally used for groups up to 24 in size.

Material required

None. Perhaps you should warn group members to wear comfortable clothes that they can move around in.

Procedure

1. Ask the participants to stand and form a circle in the centre of the training room.
2. With the participants standing in a tight circle, ask them all to raise their left hand in the air. Their right hand is now pointed to the centre of the circle. When all participants have complied with these instructions tell them to lower their left hand and grab someone else's right hand. Once this contact is made they are not allowed to break it.
3. Tell the participants that they are to untangle themselves without breaking their grip on each other. When untangled, they should again form a circle. Tell them not to worry if some of the members are facing away from the centre of the circle at the completion of the exercise.

Discussion points

1. Did anyone break contact with the person on either side?
2. Would it have been possible to complete the exercise faster? Why? Should we do it again?
3. Did anyone undertake various roles within the group?

Variation

1. Ask if any of the participants would like to wear a blindfold during the exercise. This will lead to other obvious points to cover in the debriefing.

Trainer's notes

Overview

This exercise may be used during a writing skills course or to demonstrate a decision-making process.

Goals

1. To allow participants to identify the 10 most commonly used written words in the English language.
2. To allow the group to participate in a decision-making process.
3. To energise the group.

Time required

30–60 minutes.

Size of group

Unlimited.

Material required

Prepared flipchart or overhead transparency.

Procedure

1. Tell the group members that they are going to have to decide on the top 10 words used in the written English language and that the official count has been made from a large newspaper.
2. The participants then have to decide on the 10 most commonly used words, and then the rank order of the words they select as being the most common. Give them 20–40 minutes to make their final decision.
3. After the time has lapsed, give the group feedback on their decision-making process. After the debrief has concluded they can be given the correct rankings.

Discussion points

1. How was the decision reached?
2. Who had the best logic?
3. Who sounded as if they knew the answer?
4. Who were the informal leaders? Why?

Variation

1. The group can be broken into smaller groups of 5–7 participants.

Trainer's notes

The Top Ten Words

the

of

to

and

a

in

for

is

on

that

Source
1986 counting of words from the *Sydney Morning Herald*.
Information supplied by Professor David Blair, School of
English, Macquarie University, Sydney.

20. What's Your Name?

Overview
This is a simple icebreaker designed to allow the group, as well as the facilitator, to remember everyone's names.

Goals
1. To allow participants to recall each other's names.
2. To allow the facilitator to recall all participants' names.

Time required
15–20 minutes.

Size of group
8–20 participants.

Material required
None.

Procedure
1. Tell the group members that at the end of this exercise they will hopefully know the names of all of the other participants. If name plates have been used, get the participants to turn them face down.
2. Tell the group that each person will introduce themselves by name and tell the group one unusual thing about themselves. An example could be 'My name is Jack and I have a rose garden'.
3. Then tell the group that the next person is to repeat the previous person's name and the unusual thing they told the group about themselves. That person then tells the group their name and one unusual thing about themselves.
4. The remaining participants have to follow the same procedure but recall all names and items from the first person up to the previous person.

Discussion points
1. Can everyone now remember all of the other participants' names?
2. In everyday life we have problems recalling names. This technique can be tried, but people will probably have to think of the unusual thing themselves.

Variations
1. It's best if you go first. Then the group can see what it's all about.
2. You can go last, to make certain that they have motivation to remember all of the names.
3. Name tags can be used as well with larger groups. The name tag should be covered by the participant's hand and only shown if the person trying to recall the name can't do so.

Trainer's notes

Overview

In this exercise participants see that identical objects can appear to be different in size.

Goal

1. To become aware that what you see may not be right from a perception point of view.

Time required

2–5 minutes.

Size of group

Up to 25.

Material required

2 prepared cut-outs.

Procedure

1. Ask if everyone in the group has a reasonably good idea of judging sizes.
2. The cut-outs are held up (one in each hand) so the whole group can see them. The shapes must be held in the same direction facing the group and held about 30 cm apart.
3. Ask the group to call out which of the shapes is the largest in size.
4. Then swap the shapes into the other hands and ask again which shape is the largest. This time don't expect too many people to call out.
5. Then give the shapes to the group to examine and discuss.

Discussion points

1. Why did they appear to be different sizes?
2. Was anyone manipulated at all?
3. Can everyone see that their perceptions may not always be correct?

Variation

1. You can ask for 2 volunteers to hold the shapes. After asking the group the initial question, have the volunteers swap places while still holding their shapes.

Trainer's notes

Beans

Template

Cut out two shapes from this template.
Use firm paper or light board so that they
stand rigid while being held up.

The two shapes are held in this position.

Overview

This exercise is designed to show how messages can become distorted.

Goals

1. To make participants aware of how passed on messages can become severely distorted.
2. To show participants that they need to improve their communication and listening skills.

Time required

5–10 minutes.

Size of group

Unlimited, but needs to be broken into subgroups of about 8–10 participants.

Material required

A copy of 'The Story' for each group.

Procedure

1. Tell the group that stories can get mixed up if the proper communication and listening skills are not used.
2. Break the group into subgroups of 8–10 participants. These participants sit next to each other but about a metre apart.
3. The person at the front of each subgroup is given a copy of 'The Story' to read silently.
4. After a couple of minutes they are told that they are to pass the story on (verbally, but whispering so that others can't hear) to the person next to them in the subgroup.
5. This is repeated with all of the members, one at a time passing the story they have just heard on to the next person in their subgroup.
6. When the last person in all of the subgroups has been given the final version of their story, they are to tell the total group what they have been told.

Discussion points

1. How close was the final version to the original?
2. Does this type of thing happen in the workplace?

Variations

1. You can give each subgroup a different 'story' to pass on. After each final subgroup member has told the whole group what they have been told, the first member from each subgroup should immediately read out the original version.
2. The same 'story' may be used with the whole group forming a chain of communication.
3. Take a member from each subgroup outside the training room and read them the 'story' to pass on.
4. Write a different and probably more relevant story for each training group.
5. You could give participants different levels of the organisation to represent (i.e., General Manager through to Floor Staff). If this is done, each participant could tell the group the message that they received working from the last person back to the start.

Trainer's notes

The Story

Memo to: General Manager

From: Managing Director

Tomorrow evening at approximately 7:30 pm, fireworks will be set off on the eastern side of the Sydney Harbour Bridge. This event has only taken place once before and that was on the 26 January 1988. As a token of goodwill to our employees, I would like you to arrange a bus to take all of your staff to the waterside balcony of the Sydney Opera House so that they may have spectacular views of the event. Before the fireworks commence I have arranged for one of the fireworks designers, Ms Sparky Burner, to give the staff an overview of what the fireworks signify. This will commence at 6:30 pm sharp on the balcony. In the case of rain the fireworks may be cancelled. Should this happen, please arrange to have the staff seated in the cafeteria on the first floor by 7:15 pm so that films of the previous fireworks may be shown instead.

23. Building Blocks

Overview
This is a simple exercise where everyone can see the problems of one-way communication.

Goals
1. To allow participants to observe one-way communication not working.
2. To allow participants to observe how the same scenario would have gone using two-way communication.

Time required
20–30 minutes.

Size of group
Unlimited (as long as they can all see the demonstration).

Material required
2 identically shaped sets of building blocks; some of the pairs must be different colours to allow extra confusion.

Procedure
1. Ask for a volunteer who believes he or she is a good communicator and a volunteer who believes he or she is a good listener.
2. The volunteers come to the front of the group and sit at a prepared table. The table should have a chair at each end and a screen or partition through the centre so that neither can see the other side of the table. The rest of the group should stand around the table so that they can see the different moves. Ask that they remain silent during the communication phases.
3. Give each volunteer a bag containing a set of building blocks. Tell them that they both have a set of identically shaped blocks.

4. First get the 'communicator' to build something with his or her set of blocks.
5. When that has been completed, tell the 'communicator' to give verbal instructions to the 'listener' on how to assemble exactly the same model.
6. Tell the 'listener' to follow the instructions given but not to talk back to the 'communicator'.
7. When the instructions have been completed, allow the volunteers to look at each other's models.
8. Then discussion should take place and highlight that two-way communication is essential for good communication.
9. Now get the volunteers to change roles and repeat the exercise. This time the 'listener' is to question any instructions not clearly understood. The 'communicator' should also get feedback as to what has been carried out.
10. At the conclusion the volunteers are again allowed to look at each other's models. This time they should be very similar in appearance.

Note: During debriefing you should make sure that the volunteers are not seen as being poor at these skills due to this performance.

Discussion points
1. Can we have good one-way communication?
2. What essentials are required for good communication?

Variation
1. The building blocks can be substituted with 2 sets of shaped paper cut-outs. The shapes are to be identical but a different mixture of colours should be used.

Trainer's notes

24. Put Your Jacket On

Overview
This exercise will show participants that their instructions may not be as clear as they think.

Goals
1. To allow participants to see that their instructions are not as clear as they think they are.
2. To allow participants to see how a task needs to be broken down into small segments for instructional purposes.
3. To allow participants to see that even instructions must involve two-way communication.

Time required
15–20 minutes.

Size of group
Unlimited, as long as everyone can see the demonstration.

Material required
A volunteer with a jacket or coat.

Procedure
1. Before the exercise, brief someone with a jacket or coat to help you, unknown to the rest of the group.
2. Ask for a volunteer to give someone some instructions.
3. Then ask the person with the jacket or coat to come out the front and assist. Separate the 2 participants so that they cannot see each other. Turning their backs on each other will do.
4. Tell the first volunteer to give instructions to the other person on how to remove and replace the jacket.

5. Finally inform the participants that there will be no communication between them apart from the instructions. They may now start. You will have previously told the volunteer with the jacket that they are to follow the instructions given, but to find other ways of interpreting them, for example, putting an arm in a sleeve from the cuff or putting the jacket on upside down, etc.
6. When the instructions have been finished, allow the 2 participants to turn to face each other. A discussion with the group involved should follow.
7. After the debriefing you could perform the exercise a second time, but this time allowing two-way communication. This will allow the person receiving instructions to ask questions, and for the person giving the instructions to use feedback to see if the instruction has been correctly understood.

Discussion points
1. Can instructions be given effectively using one-way communication?
2. If an instruction is not carried out correctly, who is at fault?
3. How do we check to see if an instruction has been performed correctly or not?

Variation
1. After the first demonstration, teams can be formed to devise a set of written instructions. The teams present their instructions back to the whole group.

Trainer's notes

25. Light Your Cigarette

CFMP

Overview
An exercise to show participants how difficult one-way communication can be.

Goal
1. To allow participants to see the difference between one-way and two-way communication.

Time required
10 minutes.

Size of group
Unlimited.

Material required
A packet of cigarettes and a box of matches.

Procedure
1. Ask for a volunteer who believes he or she is a good communicator and a volunteer who believes he or she is a good listener.
2. Ask the volunteers to come to the front of the group. Tell them that one is going to give the other instructions on how to light a cigarette.
3. Ask the volunteers to turn back-to-back so that they cannot see each other. Tell the person receiving the information not to ask for clarification or instruction, or ask any questions, or speak at all. Then the person giving the instructions proceeds.
4. After completion (or attempt) of the exercise, you may lead into a discussion on the requirements for giving and receiving proper instructions.

Note: During debriefing you should make sure that the volunteers are not seen as being poor at these skills due to this performance.

Discussion points
1. Why didn't the instructions work?
2. How do we rectify poorly given instructions?
3. How should we give and receive instructions so that they will work correctly?

Variations
1. Other props may be used in place of the cigarettes and matches.
2. You could take the volunteer who is receiving the instructions aside and ask him or her to follow the instructions exactly as stated, perhaps even misinterpreting some instructions without disobeying them.

Trainer's notes

26. Stepping In

Overview

This quick exercise will allow the members of the group to become more familiar with each other.

Goals

1. To allow the group to start interacting with each other.
2. To get the group moving.

Time required

5–10 minutes.

Size of group

Unlimited.

Material required

Roll of coloured tape.

Procedure

1. Stick four strips of tape to the floor before the session commences. The strips should form a square and it should be large enough for all of the group members to stand inside it.

2. At the beginning of the session point out the square on the floor and ask the participants to get inside the square, one at a time. You may prefer to make up a story as to why they have to get in it.
3. When all of the participants are inside the square ask them to step out again. Then take away one piece of tape and replace it, making the square smaller in size. Ask the participants to get inside the square again, one at a time.
4. Continue this procedure until all the participants are squeezing in and holding on to each other.

Discussion points

1. Did anyone feel uncomfortable with the exercise? Why?
2. How does everyone feel about their own personal space?
3. Do some cultures have different views?

Variations

1. Do it with group members in silence.
2. Do it blindfolded.

Trainer's notes

Overview

This card game trick can be used to show how easily people can be manipulated.

Goal

1. To allow participants to see how easy it can be to manipulate someone.

Time required

5–10 minutes.

Size of group

Unlimited.

Material required

A deck of playing cards and an envelope with a pre-selected card sealed inside it (say, the Jack of Spades).

Procedure

1. Ask everyone in the group if they are all familiar with a deck of playing cards; that is, that the deck contains 52 cards of 2 colours, 4 different suits and that there are 13 different face values.
2. Ask for a volunteer or select someone from the group to assist in the next phase of this exercise.
3. Ask the volunteer to mentally select either the red or black cards from the deck and say which they've chosen. If they select red, you ask them to mentally discard the red cards. If they say black, you ask them to keep the black cards. They are then asked to select from either the spades or the clubs. If they select clubs, you ask them to mentally discard the clubs. If they select spades, you ask them to keep the spades. Now ask them to select from the group of numbered cards (2–10) or from the picture cards. If they select the numbered cards, you ask them to mentally discard

them. If they say picture cards, you ask them to keep the picture cards. Now ask them to select from the 2 higher value picture cards (the king or ace) or from the lower 2 cards (the jack or queen). If they select the king and ace, ask them to mentally discard them. If they select the jack and queen ask them to keep them. Finally ask the volunteer to select from the queen and the jack. If they select the queen tell them to discard it. If they select the jack tell them to keep it.
4. All going to plan, the card finally left is the Jack of Spades. You now raise the sealed envelope and ask the volunteer to open the envelope. On opening the envelope, ask them to show the card that has been previously sealed inside. It is the Jack of Spades.
5. Then you can explain to the group that the volunteer has been manipulated into the selection of the desired card. Although the person made a number of selections, the facilitator did what suited the selection—to either keep or discard it.

Note: The exercise must be kept moving at a fast pace so that the group and the volunteer cannot see what is happening. If you are going to use this exercise on more than one occasion, it is best to use the same card. This reduces the chance of errors, or slow sections where you have to think about the response.

Discussion points

1. Was this a case of manipulation?
2. Do we see things like this happening in life?

Variations

1. Any card may be selected from the deck beforehand and sealed in the envelope.
2. The envelope may be given to one of the group members at the beginning of the exercise.

Trainer's notes

28. What Do People Want?

Overview
This is an exercise to let managers see that their perceptions can be different to those of their staff.

Goals
1. To let participants see that they may have different perceptions of their staff's needs.
2. To see that different groups may identify people's needs differently.

Time required
20–30 minutes.

Size of group
Unlimited.

Material required
A copy of the 'What Do People Want?' worksheet and a pen for each participant.

Procedure
1. Introduce the exercise by informing the participants that they may not really understand their staff's needs.
2. Hand out copies of the worksheet to the participants.
3. Ask them to rank the items in order of importance in the column titled 'Your Ranking', 1 being the most important and 10 the least important.
4. When they have completed that task tell them the responses gained from managers during an earlier study. Ask them to write those figures into the column titled 'Managers' Rankings'. They can now compare their results.
5. After the comparison has been made and discussed, give the participants the 'Employees' Rankings' from the earlier study. Ask them to write these figures into the appropriate column.
6. Now lead a discussion into the different perceptions.

Discussion points
1. Is anyone not surprised at the results? Why?
2. Is this a communication problem?
3. Why are the results like this?

Variation
1. To start the exercise you may ask the group 'Who knows what their staff are after?' Then go to step 2.

Study findings: What do people want?

Motivators	Managers' ranking	Employees' ranking
Money	1	5
Interesting work	5	6
Appreciation	8	1
Job security	2	4
Being an 'insider'	10	2
Promotion	3	7
Sympathy for problems	9	3
Working conditions	4	9
Loyalty from company	6	8
Tactful disciplining	7	10

Source
Unknown. Rankings from a study by Kenneth Kovach, University of Maryland, 1980.

Trainer's notes

What Do People Want?

Motivators	Your ranking	Managers' ranking	Employees' ranking
Money	_____	_____	_____
Interesting work	_____	_____	_____
Appreciation	_____	_____	_____
Job security	_____	_____	_____
Being an 'insider'	_____	_____	_____
Promotion	_____	_____	_____
Sympathy for problems	_____	_____	_____
Working conditions	_____	_____	_____
Loyalty from company	_____	_____	_____
Tactful disciplining	_____	_____	_____

Overview
This is an exercise that can be used to fill in time while waiting for latecomers.

Goal
1. To keep participants occupied while waiting for latecomers.

Time required
10 minutes.

Size of group
Unlimited.

Material required
A prepared flipchart or overhead transparency.

Procedure
1. Tell the group members that they are going to be given an exercise to do while waiting for the stragglers. You can joke about the title of this exercise being relevant to the latecomers.
2. Ask participants to imagine that they are employed by an airline. They are standing in front of the Arrivals sign at a major airport. There has been an electrical problem with the display board and they have been requested to inform the public where each flight number has come from. There is another problem with the display board as it doesn't show the first capital letter of each city.
3. Show the chart to the participants and tell them that they now have 5 minutes to prepare before the public come in to the terminal.

Trainer's notes

Discussion points
1. Did anyone get them all?
2. Isn't it amazing how some words are almost impossible to find? Why do you think this is?

Variations
1. Break the group into teams and see which team can finish first.
2. Substitute words with key words from your session and modify the story to suit.

Solution

ARRIVALS

Flight	From
050	MELBOURNE
060	CANBERRA
070	BATHURST
080	CAIRNS
090	GOVE
100	BROOME
110	WHYALLA
120	LAUNCESTON
130	SYDNEY

Arrivals

Flight	From
050	_ N O E L R E B U
060	_ B R A N E A R
070	_ T H U R S A T
080	_ S I N A R
090	_ V E O
100	_ R O M E O
110	_ H A L L A Y
120	_ N O S A T U N C E
130	_ Y E N D Y

30. **The Word Game**

Overview

This quick exercise is designed to get the group thinking about strange words within the English language.

Goals

1. To get the group warmed up after a break.
2. To make the group aware that they still have to study the English language.

Time required

10–15 minutes.

Size of group

Unlimited.

Material required

None required, but the list may be prepared on an overhead transparency or flipchart.

Procedure

1. Tell the group that the English language is full of strange words. This exercise is to get them thinking about some of those words.
2. Either show or give a prepared list to the participants. Tell them to find the strange words that you are describing.

3. Declare the person that gets the most right the winner.

Discussion points

1. How many did each person find?
2. How do we find out about these words?

Variations

1. Teams may be formed to solve the complete list.
2. You may find other strange words to use.

Source

Adapted from 'Weird Words', *Oddities in Words, Pictures and Figures*, Reader's Digest Services Pty Limited, Sydney, 1975.

Solution

1. Facetious
2. Rhythms
3. Bookkeeper
4. Catchphrase
5. Strengthlessness

Trainer's notes

Strange Words

1. Which reasonably common 9-letter word contains all 5 vowels in the right sequence and only used once each?

2. What 7-letter word doesn't contain any of the 5 vowels?

3. What word contains 3 consecutive pairs of letters in it?

4. What word has the letters TCHPHR grouped together in the middle of it?

5. What 16-letter word only uses E as a vowel?

31. Spelling Bee

Overview
This quick exercise tests spelling ability.

Goals
1. To test the group's spelling competency.
2. To energise the group.

Time required
10–15 minutes.

Size of group
Unlimited.

Material required
A prepared overhead or flipchart containing the words shown overleaf and a pen and paper for each participant.

Procedure
1. Tell the group members that they are going to have a 5-minute spelling test.
2. Tell them that you are about to show them a list of 20 words and that half of them are spelt incorrectly. Also tell them that this particular list was compiled after tests on 87 000 schoolchildren between the ages of 13 and 18.
3. Ask them to identify the 10 words that have been incorrectly spelt and write down the correct spelling.
4. Display the list for 5 minutes and discuss when completed.

Discussion points
1. Does anyone feel that they have the 10 correct answers?
2. Why are these words sometimes awkward to spell?

Variation
1. You may break the group into teams to discuss each word and identify the ones that have been incorrectly spelt. The team should agree on the words and the correct spelling. Each team then reports its findings back to the whole group.

Source
Adapted from 'Spelling Bees That Really Sting', *Oddities in Words, Pictures and Figures*, Reader's Digest Services Pty Limited, Sydney, 1975.

Solution

Separate (c)	Until	All right
Ceiling (c)	Address	Correspondence (c)
Schedule (c)	Accommodate (c)	Development
Parliament	Besiege (c)	Bicycle (c)
Weird	Acquire (c)	Misspelled
Possess (c)	Restaurant	Embarrassed (c)
Truly	Receive	

(c) indicates that the original word was correct.

Trainer's notes

Spelling Bee

Separate	Untill	Alright
Ceiling	Adress	Correspondence
Schedule	Accommodate	Developement
Parlament	Besiege	Bicycle
Wierd	Acquire	Mispelled
Possess	Resteraunt	Embarrassed
Truely	Recieve	

32. **Another Spelling Bee**

Overview
This is another quick exercise to test spelling ability.

Goals
1. To test the group's spelling competency.
2. To energise the group.

Time required
15–20 minutes.

Size of group
Unlimited.

Material required
A prepared overhead or flipchart containing the words shown overleaf and a pen and paper for each participant.

Procedure
1. Tell the group members that they are going to have a 10-minute spelling test.
2. Tell them that you are about to show them a list of 40 words and that half of them are spelt incorrectly. Also tell them this list was compiled from words that baffle teachers and writers.
3. Ask them to identify the 20 words that have been incorrectly spelt and write down the correct spelling.
4. Display the list for 10 minutes and discuss when completed.

Discussion points
1. Does anyone feel that they have the 20 correct answers?
2. Why are these words sometimes awkward to spell?

Variation
1. You may break the group into teams to discuss each word and identify the ones that have been incorrectly spelt. The team should agree on the words and the correct spelling. Each team then reports its findings back to the whole group.

Source
Adapted from 'Spelling Bees That Really Sting', *Oddities in Words, Pictures and Figures*, Reader's Digest Services Pty Limited, Sydney, 1985.

Solution

Accelerator (c)	Immaculate	Propeller
Allotted (c)	Innocuous (c)	Raspberry
Assassin	Liquefy	Rhinoceros
Category (c)	Millionaire (c)	Sheriff
Connoisseur	Miscellaneous	Sieve (c)
Demagogue (c)	Paraffin (c)	Solder (c)
Desiccate	Paralysis (c)	Tariff (c)
Dilapidated (c)	Pedagogue (c)	Tonsillitis
Discriminate	Penitentiary	Tyranny (c)
Dishevelled	Perspiration (c)	Vacillate
Dissipate	Phlegm	Vanilla (c)
Effervescent (c)	Picnicking	Victuals (c)
Fuselage (c)	Prairie (c)	
Gaiety	Prescription	

(c) indicates that the original word was correct.

Trainer's notes

Another Spelling Bee

Accelerator	Immacculate	Propellor
Allotted	Innocuous	Rasberry
Assasin	Liquify	Rinoceros
Category	Millionaire	Sherriff
Connoiseur	Miscellanious	Sieve
Demagogue	Paraffin	Solder
Dessicate	Paralysis	Tariff
Dilapidated	Pedagogue	Tonsilitis
Discrimanate	Penitenciary	Tyranny
Disheveled	Perspiration	Vaccillate
Disippate	Phlem	Vanilla
Effervescent	Picknicking	Victuals
Fuselage	Prairie	
Gaity	Presciption	

33. Team Task No. 1

Overview
This exercise gives teams a problem to solve.

Goals
1. To get the group's members working together as teams.
2. To see which members take up the different group functions. (This will probably be a hidden goal at the beginning of the exercise.)

Time required
30–40 minutes.

Size of group
Up to 24; becomes too hard to observe with larger numbers.

Material required
A copy of the 'Numbers Puzzle' and a pen for each team.

Procedure
1. This exercise is best used when dealing with the topics of teams, meetings or similar. Introduce the topic and break the group into teams of 5–7 members each. If extra members are available they may be used as observers.
2. Give each team a copy of the 'Numbers Puzzle' and a pen. Place this material in the centre of the team; don't give it directly to any one member.
3. Tell the teams that they have a problem to solve. They have to divide the square on their puzzle into four equal parts, each part containing one of each number.

4. After the teams have completed the problem you (and observers if used) give feedback on the roles that the individual team members performed.

Discussion points
1. Did the team members see others performing various roles?
2. Were these roles predictable for each person?
3. Can these roles be seen in the workplace?
4. Can we modify our roles to suit?

Variations
1. A time limit may be set.
2. Various members may be targeted for the chairperson's role and handed the puzzle and pen.

Solution

3	2	1	1
3	1	4	3
4	3	2	4
2	2	1	4

Trainer's notes

Numbers Puzzle

3	**2**	**1**	**1**
3	**1**	**4**	**3**
4	**3**	**2**	**4**
2	**2**	**1**	**4**

Instructions: Divide this square into four equal parts. Each part must contain one of each number shown.

34. **Team Task No. 2**

Overview
This exercise gives teams a problem to solve.

Goals
1. To get the group's members working together as teams.
2. To see which members take up the different group functions. (This will probably be a hidden goal at the beginning of the exercise.)

Time required
30–40 minutes.

Size of group
Up to 24; becomes too hard to observe with larger numbers.

Material required
A prepared overhead or flipchart with the final shape shown, several rectangular sheets of paper and a pair of scissors for each team.

Procedure
1. This exercise is best used when dealing with the topics of teams, meetings or similar. Introduce the topic and break the group into teams of 5–7 members each. If extra members are available they may be used as observers.
2. Give each team several sheets of blank paper and a pair of scissors. Place this material in the centre of the team; don't give it directly to any one member.
3. Tell the teams that they have a problem to solve. They have to finish up with a shape the same as the one shown. They are only allowed to make one cut with the scissors and it must be a straight cut.

4. After the teams have completed the problem you (and observers if used) give feedback on the roles that the individual team members performed.

Discussion points
1. Did the members work as a team?
2. Did the team members see others performing various roles?

Variations
1. A time limit may be set.
2. Various members may be targeted for the chairperson's role and handed the sheets of paper and the scissors.

Solution

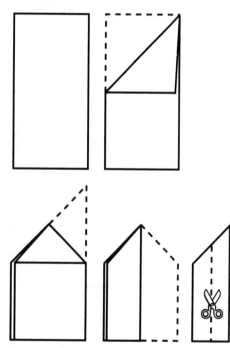

Trainer's notes

The Final Shape

Instructions: Making only one straight cut with your scissors you must finish up with the shape shown above.

40. The Numbers Game

Overview
This exercise will show participants how practice improves learning.

Goals
1. To allow participants to see how practice improves learning.
2. To get the group thinking about student practice and evaluation.

Time required
10–15 minutes.

Size of group
Unlimited, but becomes administratively difficult with groups larger than 12–18 people.

Material required
A pen and 6 copies of 'The Numbers Game' handout for each participant. A watch with a second hand and a flipchart or whiteboard are also required.

Procedure
1. Give each participant a pen and 6 copies of 'The Numbers Game' handout. Place the handouts face down and ask the participants to leave them face down until asked to turn them over.
2. Tell the group that they are going to participate in an experiment involving 'student practice'. Tell them that the handouts they have been given contain 80 consecutive numbers (1 to 80). Number 1 has been circled to show them where they start. Tell them they will be given 1 minute after they are told to turn their sheet over to use their pen to connect as many consecutive numbers as they can, starting at number 1. At the end of the minute they are to turn their sheet face down again and wait for the next instruction.
3. Ask the participants to write number 1 on the back of the first handout. Now tell them to turn the sheets over and join the numbers. Stop them after 1 minute and ask them to turn their sheets face down.
4. Now ask the participants to write number 2 on the back of the second sheet. Repeat the exercise. Continue this for all 6 handouts.
5. Now ask the participants to advise what number they got up to on the first trial. Display this information on the whiteboard or flipchart. Repeat this for the following trials.
6. It will be obvious that each member's scores have improved over the 6 trials. If time permits, you may total all of the individual trials to give a better comparison.

Note: The pattern starts with number 1 in the top left-hand quadrant. The numbers then rotate to the top right quadrant, the bottom left quadrant, the bottom right quadrant back to the top left quadrant. This pattern is repeated for all 80 numbers.

Discussion points
1. Why did the scores improve?
2. Did anyone's scores not improve? Why?
3. Did anyone find the pattern in the location of the numbers?
4. Can we use this experience in our training sessions?
5. How much practice should we allow/insist of our students?

Variation
1. The number of sheets may be decreased or increased to suit group needs and time constraints.

Source
Adapted from 'The Numbers Game', John W. Newstrom and Edward E. Scannell, *Games Trainers Play*, McGraw-Hill, Inc., New York, 1980.

Trainer's notes

The Numbers Game

45

42

①

21

37

22

26

10

33

30

62

70

46

61

6

65

29

5

14

2

41

58

53

57

77

38

78

74

69

66

13

17

25

50

18

54

73

49

9

34

67

23

43

27

8

40

32

68

44

7

31

56

19

59

60

16

39

63

12

64

35

36

3

75

24

4

47

55

15

72

76

52

11

28

79

71

51

20

80

48

Overview
This exercise is a tension-relieving energiser.

Goal
1. To allow participants to unwind.

Time required
5 minutes.

Size of group
Unlimited.

Material required
None.

Procedure
1. Tell the group members that they are all going to become marionettes. The participants are to sit in their chairs and in response to your instructions perform simple movements such as crossing their legs or standing up. You should demonstrate a simple task.

2. After each participant has practised being a marionette give them more complicated routines to perform. This can include tasks such as getting on a bike, walking around the room, dancing with each other, etc.

Discussion point
1. Is this how people feel sometimes at work?

Variations
1. Have participants act out secret routines and have the rest of the group guess.
2. Use the marionette concept with charades.

Source
Adapted from 'Pulling Strings', Nancy Loving Tubesing and Donald A. Tubesing, *Structured Exercises in Stress Management*, Volume 1, Whole Person Press, Duluth MN, 1983.

Trainer's notes

42. No Laughing

Overview
This exercise is designed to add a little laughter to the session.

Goal
1. To get all of the participants laughing.

Time required
5 minutes.

Size of group
Up to 16.

Material required
None.

Procedure
1. Get the group members to form a circle, either sitting or standing.
2. Give them the instruction that one participant will start with a word and pass it on to the participant sitting on their right.
3. When that participant receives the word they must repeat it twice to the participant on their right.
4. That participant must then pass the word on to the participant on their right saying it three times, and so on.
5. After the instructions have been given, the first participant is given the word 'HA' to start the exercise. Ask the group to treat this exercise seriously and not to laugh.

Discussion points
1. Why did everyone start laughing?
2. What would have happened had we used a more frightening word?

Variations
1. Substitute the word with any other humorous word.
2. You can establish a chain where the current participant says 'HA' and it must be echoed back along the line.

Source
Adapted from 'Ha', Sue Forbess-Greene, *The Encyclopedia of Icebreakers*, University Associates, California, 1983.

Trainer's notes

43. Shuffling Papers

Overview
This is a quick team exercise with competition.

Goals
1. To get team members interacting with each other.
2. To identify the group leaders.

Time required
10–20 minutes.

Size of group
Unlimited, but needs to be broken into subgroups of 6–8 participants.

Material required
A newspaper or magazine for each group (all of the same number of pages) and a small prize for the winning group.

Procedure
1. Tell the participants that they are to break into subgroups of 6–8 participants.
2. When the teams have been formed, give each a complete newspaper or magazine (with the staples removed) that has had all of the pages shuffled up.

3. The team's task is to sort all of the sheets into the correct order. The first team finished is the winner.

Discussion points
1. Did a leader emerge in each team?
2. Was the leader elected or did he or she just take over?
3. Was the leader effective?
4. How did the leader like having the role?
5. How did the other individuals feel about the leadership role?

Variations
1. You could cut the page numbers off the papers. If the page numbers are cut off, be sure to allow more time for the exercise.
2. Use a lengthy document from the organisation instead of the newspaper.

Source
Adapted from 'Newspaper Shuffle', Sue Forbess-Greene, *The Encyclopedia of Icebreakers*, University Associates, California, 1983.

Trainer's notes

44. Cleaning Up

Overview
This is a fast-moving game that will get the group laughing.

Goals
1. To build team spirit.
2. To allow participants to use problem-solving skills.
3. To get the blood circulating after a long session.

Time required
10–15 minutes.

Size of group
Up to 24.

Material required
Sufficient quantities of flipchart paper.

Procedure
1. Ask the group to break into teams of 6–8 participants. All teams must be the same size. If there will be participants left over, you should nominate referees beforehand. Ask the team members to take their shoes off for this exercise.
2. Give each team a number of sheets of flipchart paper. The number of sheets should be half that of the team size.
3. Mark a starting line at one end of the training room. Position a chair for each team at the other end of the training room.

4. Now tell the teams that they will be involved in a race. They are to start at the starting line by placing one sheet of flipchart paper on the floor and having one participant stand on it. That participant then places another sheet down in front of them and moves onto it. The second team member then moves onto the first sheet and so on. It will soon become apparent to the participants that they have to share spaces on the sheets of paper.
5. The first team to go around their chair and get back to the starting line will be declared the winner. If any of the team members walks on the floor and not the paper, the team has to go back to the beginning and start again.

Note: Participants can solve this in a number of ways (by moving the back sheet of paper, by ripping the paper into strips, etc.) so this can also be used as an exercise in lateral thinking.

Discussion points
1. Did the winning team perform like a team?
2. Why didn't the other teams do as well?

Variations
1. Smaller sheets of paper may be used.
2. A larger circuit may be established.

Trainer's notes

45. What Do You See?

Overview
This exercise shows how people perceive things differently.

Goal
1. To allow participants to see that everyone doesn't perceive things the same way.

Time required
5 minutes.

Size of group
Unlimited.

Material required
An overhead transparency of the 'Old Woman/Young Woman'.

Procedure
1. Project the transparency onto a screen and ask the participants to look at the image for a few seconds. Tell them that they are looking for a picture of an old or young woman.
2. Ask them to raise their hands if they can see only the old woman. Next the participants are asked to raise their hands if they only see the young woman. Finally they are asked to raise their hands if they can see both the old and young woman.
3. Now show them where both of these women are in the picture. Alternatively get one of the participants to show them.

Discussion points
1. Why do we perceive things differently?
2. Why can't some people see both women? Even after being shown where they are?
3. How can we improve our perception skills?

Variation
1. The material may be given as a handout if an overhead projector is not available.

Source
Adapted from 'Old Woman/Young Woman', John W. Newstrom and Edward E. Scannell, *Games Trainers Play*, McGraw-Hill, Inc., New York, 1980, and Edwin G. Boring, 'A New Ambiguous Figure', *American Journal of Psychology*, July 1930, p. 444. (Originally drawn by cartoonist W. E. Hill, published in *Puck*, 6 November 1915.)

Trainer's notes

What Do You See?

46. Smile

 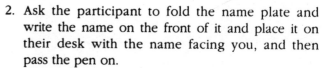

Overview
This name plate and rules exercise can be used for any training session.

Goal
1. To let the participants know your ground rules.

Time required
2–5 minutes.

Size of group
Unlimited.

Material required
A printed name plate for each participant and a marking pen.

Procedure
1. Hand out a name plate to each participant. Also give one participant the marking pen.

2. Ask the participant to fold the name plate and write the name on the front of it and place it on their desk with the name facing you, and then pass the pen on.
3. Then ask someone to read out the rules for you.

Discussion points
1. Ask if anyone has any questions regarding the points shown.
2. You could also ask if there are any other rules that participants would like to see included for this program.

Variation
1. If any type of introduction exercise is to be done, the name plates may be used to mix or pair up participants at random.

Trainer's notes

Name:

SMILE

This training is for you.
Here are a few tips to ensure its success.

* Participate in discussions
* Listen to the other viewpoint
* Say what you think
* Keep discussion on the subject
* Be patient with other members
* Try to relate your experiences
* Ask questions, other members would also like to know

Name:

SMILE

This training is for you.
Here are a few tips to ensure its success.

* Participate in discussions
* Listen to the other viewpoint
* Say what you think
* Keep discussion on the subject
* Be patient with other members
* Try to relate your experiences
* Ask questions, other members would also like to know

47. Stress Budget

Overview
This is a simple exercise to get participants to look at their allocation of resources to problems.

Goals
1. To make participants aware of the resources they use on problems.
2. To get the participants to re-allocate their resources to better ratios.

Time required
10–15 minutes.

Size of group
Unlimited.

Material required
A dollar's worth of small change for each participant.

Procedure
1. Tell the group members that they are going to be able to budget resources against their problems. Before they start, however, they are to identify both the major and minor problems that they encounter on a daily basis.
2. After the participants have each identified a list of problems, give each member a dollar's worth of loose change.
3. Now tell the participants that they are to allocate amounts of money to the problems they have identified. The amounts are to represent the amount of time they spend each day on that particular problem.
4. When that has been completed, tell them to record the values that they have put on each individual problem.
5. The next step is to tell them to allocate what they think would be a more logical investment of their time and resources to each problem.
6. They should record the new amounts and compare them with the original amounts. The re-allocation of these resources should be discussed and participants should note what changes they will make on completion of this training.

Discussion points
1. How much did the 2 amounts differ?
2. Was anyone not surprised at the differences?
3. Could this type of exercise be used regularly back in the workplace?

Variations
1. The exercise can be done in small groups with the participants discussing each other's allocation of resources.
2. Each participant can be asked to report back to the whole group.

Trainer's notes

48. **Negotiation**

Overview

This exercise will get participants involved in different methods of negotiation.

Goals

1. To introduce the topic of negotiation.
2. To start to get the group warmed up.
3. To allow participants to try their current negotiation skills.

Time required

10 minutes.

Size of group

Unlimited.

Material required

A dollar coin for each pair of participants.

Procedure

1. Ask the group members to form pairs, preferably with someone they don't know.

2. Give each pair a dollar coin between them.
3. Tell them that they have exactly 5 minutes to decide between them who is going to get the dollar coin. The only rules are that they are not allowed physical contact (violence) during the discussion period. If they cannot decide who is to collect the dollar coin, it is to be returned to you.
4. When the time is up you can lead into a discussion on negotiation and decision-making techniques.

Discussion points

1. What type of techniques were used by the group?
2. Were all of the negotiations honest?
3. How did people feel about a time limit being imposed?

Variations

1. Use a different value coin or notes.
2. Use some other type of object that the individuals would be prepared to negotiate for.

Trainer's notes

49. Our Greatest Fears

Overview
This icebreaker will allow participants to recognise that they are not the only people with a fear of public speaking.

Goals
1. To get the group warmed up to the topic.
2. To allow participants to recognise that they are not the only ones with a fear of public speaking.

Time required
15–20 minutes.

Size of group
Up to 24.

Material required
A sheet of paper and a pen for each subgroup, and a prepared overhead of 'The Ten Worst Human Fears'.

Procedure
1. Ask the participants to break into subgroups of 5–7 members and give each subgroup a sheet of paper and a pen.
2. Ask the subgroups to use their imagination and list what they would consider to be the 10 worst fears identified by the general public in a random survey. The subgroups are given 10 minutes to draw up their lists.
3. After the subgroups have completed their lists, ask each subgroup to present its finding. You could write these up on the whiteboard.
4. After all responses have been obtained, use the prepared overhead to reveal the list compiled by David Wallechinsky. These items should be revealed one at a time from the bottom up.
5. At the conclusion reinforce to the participants that they are not by themselves with the fears they may have regarding the course they are about to undertake.

Discussion points
1. Which subgroup came closest to the prepared list?
2. Did anyone expect these results?
3. Would there be any difference in the results in different countries?

Variations
1. This exercise could be done on an individual basis.
2. It could be done as one large group with the facilitator soliciting participant responses.

Source
Adapted from 'The Worst Human Fears (in the US)', John W. Newstrom and Edward E. Scannell, *Games Trainers Play*, McGraw-Hill, Inc., New York, 1980, and David Wallechinsky et al., *The Book of Lists*, Wm Morrow & Co., Inc., New York, 1987.

Trainer's notes

The Ten Worst Human Fears (in the US)

1. Speaking before a group
2. Heights
3. Insects and bugs
4. Financial problems
5. Deep water
6. Sickness
7. Death
8. Flying
9. Loneliness
10. Dogs

50. Marooned

Overview
This is an icebreaker to get the participants to identify their favourite characters or people they would like to be with.

Goals
1. To get the participants to select people they respect.
2. To make the participants more aware of each other's perceptions.

Time required
10–15 minutes.

Size of group
Unlimited.

Material required
A piece of paper and a pen for each participant.

Procedure
1. Ask the participants to imagine that they have just been marooned on a desert island.
2. Now give each participant a sheet of paper and a pen.
3. Tell them that this is an unusual island, in that they can select 6 well-known personalities to be marooned with. They have 5 minutes to select the 6 people and write their names on the paper.
4. After that has been completed, get each group member in turn to tell the rest of the group their selection and the reasons for making such a selection.

Discussion points
1. Did anyone have trouble trying to reduce their list to 6?
2. Did anyone have trouble in not finding enough people to be marooned with?
3. Now that they have heard everyone else's selections, would anyone like to change their list?

Variations
1. Television personalities may be substituted for well-known people.
2. People within your organisation may be substituted for well-known personalities.

Trainer's notes

Overview

This exercise is an icebreaker or energiser that may be used any time during the program.

Goals

1. To allow participants to show what they feel about certain issues.
2. To get participants moving around.

Time required

10–15 minutes.

Size of group

Up to 24.

Material required

A set of 3 signs with one marked 'Strongly Agree', another marked 'Undecided', and the last marked 'Strongly Disagree'.

Procedure

1. Place the signs along the full length of one of the walls in the training room, with 'Strongly Agree' and 'Strongly Disagree' at opposite ends, and 'Undecided' in the middle.
2. Now instruct the participants that as a statement is made each individual must stand somewhere along the wall indicating their feeling or belief about the statement.
3. Now read out a statement from a prepared list of current controversial or topical statements.

Discussion points

1. How did everyone feel about having to take a public stance?
2. Did anyone find that they purposely didn't allow themselves to go to either extreme with others watching? Why?

Variations

1. The participants could be given a chance to tell why they selected the position they did.
2. The statements could be related to the organisation if they are all members of the same group.

Trainer's notes

Strongly Agree

- -

Strongly Disagree

- -

Undecided

Overview

This exercise is designed to get participants moving and working as a team.

Goals

1. To allow participants the chance to work as a team.
2. To get the group moving.
3. To participate in a number of decision-making processes.
4. To see how competitive most people are.

Time required

15–30 minutes.

Size of group

Unlimited.

Material required

A packet of balloons.

Procedure

1. Tell the group that they are going to participate in a new game called 'Balloon Ball'. The object of this game is to score as many goals as possible in the time allowed. The group is divided into 2 smaller teams. The teams also have to decide what the goals are (opposite walls are fine). A goal is scored by hitting the designated wall with the balloon. They also have to inflate the balloons. More than one may be required as they tend to break easily.

2. After the group has divided into 2 smaller teams they should decide which way they each want to face. After that decision has been made the team members should position themselves in a scattered manner around the room. Once people decide on a position, they are not allowed to move from it until the end of the exercise.

3. Tell the group when to commence play. Scores are to be kept by the participants. At the conclusion of the exercise a discussion should follow.

Note: The original instruction asked the participants to score as many goals as possible. Did the teams compete with each other, or did they work together? If they worked together the score will be high as they will not have been trying to compete with each other. Most people tend to see that they are competing at everything.

Discussion points

1. Was teamwork used effectively? Why? Why not?
2. What was the final score?
3. Is this an acceptable score? (See Note in Procedure.)

Variations

1. Other types of balls may be used for different effects.
2. More than one balloon can be used at once.

Trainer's notes

Overview

This exercise may be used for introductions. It can also be modified to fit into other stages of training.

Goals

1. To get to know each other.
2. To allow the participants to label their own pace.

Time required

10 minutes.

Size of group

Up to 16.

Material required

3 signs marked 'Tortoise', 'Hare' and 'Thoroughbred'.

Procedure

1. Start the session by quickly checking to see if everyone remembers the story of the tortoise and the hare.
2. Introduce the exercise as an icebreaker. Tell the participants to listen carefully to the descriptions of the tortoise, hare and thoroughbred. Then read out the descriptions.
3. Stick the 3 signs on the wall and ask the participants to move to the sign that best describes them.
4. After all participants have selected a location, tell them to introduce themselves to the rest of the group and state why they chose that description of themselves.

Discussion point

1. Do people always fit into the same category or do they change with different people and situations?

Variation

1. The participants can be asked to create a list of good and bad points for each of the categories.

Trainer's notes

Each participant during the introduction may be required to add the points that they raise to a flipchart.

Source

Adapted from 'Tortoise, Hare or Thoroughbred', Nancy Loving Tubesing and Donald A. Tubesing, *Structured Exercises in Stress Management*, Volume 2, Whole Person Press, Duluth MN, 1983.

The descriptions

Tortoise

Likes to move ahead slowly and steadily.
Won't be rushed.
Finds strength from pulling in head.
Has a strong protective shell.
Doesn't take unnecessary risks.
Prefers life on an even keel without crisis.
Sets own pace, takes one thing at a time.

Hare

Moves with quick starts and stops.
Produces well under pressure.
Finds strength in exploration and challenge.
Is fragile, agile and lucky.
Enjoys risks and adventures.
Hops from crisis to crisis, is easily distracted.
Always has many irons in the fire.

Thoroughbred

Economy and grace of movement.
Varies pace according to situation.
Strength comes from top-flight conditioning.
Always under control.
Thrives on competition and challenge.
Has clear goals with mileposts to mark progress.
Always has something left for the stretch.

TORTOISE

HARE

THOROUGHBRED

54. Where Are We Now?

ITCFP

Overview
This exercise can be used at the beginning of a day on a program of longer duration.

Goals
1. To allow participants an opportunity to mix with each other and find out what has happened to each other since the last meeting.
2. To allow participants to participate in a team-building exercise.
3. To allow participants a chance to get to know each other a little better.

Time required
30–60 minutes, depending on the size of the group.

Size of group
Up to 18.

Material required
None.

Procedure
1. Ask the group members to break into pairs. Tell them to talk to each other and find out what significant things have happened since they last met. This should take 10 minutes.
2. After they have finished these discussions ask everyone in the group to form a circle with their chairs and be seated.
3. Now ask the group members to share the things that have happened to them with the rest of the group. Each person is to speak about the person they were talking to, not themselves. Ask for a volunteer to start and finish with yourself, as facilitator.

Discussion points
1. Did anyone feel threatened by the exercise? Why?
2. Do members now feel a little more like a team? Why? Why not?
3. Should team members share these thoughts? Why? Why not?

Variations
1. You may decide to talk first.
2. Names can be drawn for the order.

Trainer's notes

Overview

This exercise will give participants an idea on how to control their nerves. It can be used in conjunction with Exercise 49, 'Our Greatest Fears'.

Goals

1. To allow participants to see different ways of relaxing.
2. To allow participants a chance to see how others control their fears of public speaking.

Time required

10 minutes.

Size of group

Unlimited.

Material required

A copy of the 'Dealing with Nerves' handout for each participant.

Procedure

1. Tell the group that all public speakers have some fears and suffer from nerves.

2. Ask the group members for suggestions for controlling nerves. List all ideas on a whiteboard and discuss or explain them.
3. Read through the points covered in the handout. Discuss and explain these as necessary.
4. After all the points have been covered, give a copy of the handout to each participant.

Discussion point

1. Has anyone ever tried any of these methods?

Variations

1. Get the participants to prepare individual lists.
2. Break into teams of 5–7 members and allow them to design their own lists for discussion. After the teams have presented their findings carry on at point 3.

Source

Adapted from 'Difficult Situations and Nerves', Gary Kroehnert, *Basic Training for Trainers*, McGraw-Hill Book Company Australia, Sydney, 1990.

Trainer's notes

Dealing with Nerves

1. Be at ease and relax. They want to listen to you.
2. Breathe deeply as you walk towards the venue.
3. Mentally rehearse the sequence of your presentation.
4. Use the self-fulfilling prophecy.
5. Arrive early so that you can settle in.
6. Dress the part and look professional.
7. Try to anticipate questions.
8. Check all of your support equipment beforehand.
9. Create a physical setting you feel comfortable with.
10. Use your prepared session notes.
11. Establish credibility at the beginning of your presentation.
12. Give your audience an outline of the events and topics.
13. Motivate the group to want to listen to you.
14. Use brainteasers as an opening.
15. Practise your session beforehand.
16. Use your tension to enhance your performance.
17. Move around.
18. Warm your voice up before starting.
19. Keep eye contact with all of your audience.
20. Be comfortable with the arrangement of your resources.
21. Practise with your training aids.
22. Research and know your topic.
23. Use unobtrusive isometric exercises.
24. Attend appropriate presentation or public speaking courses.
25. Remember your audience's attention span.
26. Use all of the principles of adult learning.
27. Find out in advance who your participants are.
28. Admit your mistakes, but only if you make them.
29. Always appear to be enthusiastic.
30. Use a video or tape recorder to evaluate your performance.
31. Develop your own style of presentation.
32. Get feedback from your audience.
33. Don't read from the text.
34. Don't have a heavy night before a day of presentations.

Overview

This exercise shows how to use one form of memory jogger.

Goals

1. To show participants that memory joggers do work.
2. To act as a tension reliever at the beginning of training.

Time required

10–15 minutes.

Size of group

Unlimited.

Material required

A sheet of paper, a pen and a copy of the 'Mind Map' handout for each participant and a flipchart.

Procedure

1. Ask the group members if they know of any methods to increase recall abilities. A quick discussion may follow.
2. Ask the participants to think of things they may want to remember, such as a shopping list. Ask volunteers to come forward and write their selected item on the flipchart. They are to come up with a list of 12 items.
3. Tear off the flipchart paper and fold it. Now continue the session normally.
4. After a couple of hours, give participants a pen and paper each and ask them to write down the 12 selected items in the correct order, without assistance from other group members. Allow a couple of minutes for this attempt.
5. Find out who has all 12 in the correct order. It is unlikely that any participant will have them all. Now is your chance to show them your powers of recall. Ask them to call out any number between 1 and 12. As a number is called out you should write it on the flipchart (in the correct sequence) and write the original item that had been placed beside that number. When all 12 have been written on the flipchart compare this to the original list and discuss the results.
6. After the discussion tell the group how you did it and give out a copy of the handout.

Discussion points

1. How appropriate is this to people's needs?
2. Does anyone else know of other methods?

Source

Peter Cross, Kingsford, NSW.

Trainer's notes

Mind Map

You must be able to remember these key words before using this method of recall. To remember any 12 items in the correct sequence you have to follow these instructions. As each item is given to you it is essential that you picture the key word for the associated number and its instructions.

Key words

1.	**Bun**	5.	**Drive**	9.	**Dine**
2.	**Glue**	6.	**Mix**	10.	**Pen**
3.	**Key**	7.	**Heaven**	11.	**Devon**
4.	**Store**	8.	**Ape**	12.	**Shelves**

1. **BUN** ... imagine your favourite hamburger ... the object you are trying to remember is inside it ... you take a bite and bite on the object.

2. **GLUE** ... imagine a pot of glue ... you find yourself painting glue over the object, you put so much on that your hands get stuck to the object and you can't shake it off.

3. **KEY** ... imagine yourself opening a cupboard door with a key and the object falls out, multiple objects, and you can't stop them, they build up around you.

4. **STORE** ... you are in your favourite corner store and all of the shelves are filled with the object ... you load a shopping trolley so full with the object that it overflows onto the floor ... you keep picking them up but they keep falling.

5. **DRIVE** ... you are speeding down the road when the object (gigantic in size) appears ahead ... you slam on the brakes but still hit the object hard smashing it to pieces ... some of the pieces smash through the windscreen and hit you in the face.

6. **MIX** ... you are mixing the object (multiple) in a bowl ... you keep mixing faster and faster until the objects start falling out ... you see yourself picking them up and putting them back in ... but they keep falling out.

7. **HEAVEN** ... you see in front of you an escalator heading up to heaven with Saint Peter at the top beckoning you to come up ... you try to get up the escalator but you are stopped by hundreds of the object coming down ... you see and feel yourself slipping and falling over ... you can't make it.

8. **APE** ... you are at a zoo looking through the bars at an ape ... the floor of the cage is covered with the object ... you are laughing at the ape and it gets angry and starts throwing the objects at you ... one of the objects gets through the bars and hits you in the face.

9. **DINE** ... you are seated at your favourite restaurant with an empty plate ... suddenly the object appears on the plate ... you try to cut it with your knife and fork.

10. **PEN** ... picture the object ... you pick up a great big pen with red ink in it ... you must see yourself writing the name of the object on the object itself with the red ink from the pen.

11. **DEVON** ... imagine a big nob of devon ... you cut it in half and the object is inside it.

12. **SHELVES** ... you walk into a storeroom at home ... there are shelves everywhere ... the shelves are packed with the object ... they start falling off the shelves on top of you.

Extra tips
- You must picture each step in your mind before you move on.
- Colour helps bring immediate recall.
- Exaggeration is great. Big objects may be small or small objects may be large.

57. Say What?

Overview
This is an exercise where participants have to deal with language problems.

Goals
1. To examine language problems relative to communication.
2. To let participants feel frustration due to language barriers.

Time required
90–120 minutes.

Size of group
Unlimited, but needs to be broken into subgroups of 5–7 participants.

Material required
A sheet of paper, a pen and a blindfold for each participant.

Procedure
1. Inform the group that they are going to participate in a communication exercise. Break the group into subgroups of 5–7 people.
2. Now tell the subgroups that they are each to create a new language. The new language must have at least an introduction, descriptions for objects within the room, a positive comment, a negative comment, and a farewell. Give the subgroups 30 minutes to design and learn their new languages.
3. After the 30-minute period ask the subgroup members to pair off with someone from another subgroup. When the pairs have been formed tell them that they now have 15 minutes each to teach each other their language. Also tell them that they are only to use their new language and not to speak in another dialect.
4. At the conclusion of this stage ask all of the participants to put their blindfolds on. Tell them that with blindfolds in position they are to now form into their original subgroups. For this phase they are again only to use their newly created language.

Discussion points
1. How did people feel during the exercise?
2. What did the exercise highlight about communication?
3. How well did people learn the other participant's language?

Variation
1. For the final grouping the participants can be asked to form into groups only using the language that they have been taught in point 3.

Source
Adapted from 'Babel: Interpersonal Communication', J. William Pfeiffer and John E. Jones, *A Handbook of Structured Experiences for Human Relations Training*, Volume 5, University Associates, California, 1975.

Trainer's notes

58. Room 703

Overview
This is a problem-solving exercise that is team oriented.

Goals
1. To look at group strategies for problem-solving.
2. To see how competition affects the problem-solving process.
3. To see how group members pass on information.

Time required
45–60 minutes.

Size of group
Unlimited.

Material required
A sheet of paper and a pen for each participant and a set of prepared 'Information Cards' for each team.

Procedure
1. Break the group into teams of 6 members each. Any extras can be used as observers.
2. Give members in every team one of the 'Room 703 Information cards' and allow 2 minutes to read and study the information on their own card. Note that each card is identified by the number of dots after the first sentence.
3. After the 2-minute period tell the teams to begin working. They have 20 minutes for this phase.
4. After all team members have reached agreement about the solution, lead into a discussion on how the task was achieved and what techniques were used for problem-solving.

Note: The six cards make up a complete set for each team. Each of the cards is identified by the number of dots after the first sentence. This enables you to be sure you give each team a complete set of instructions.

Trainer's notes

Discussion points
1. What was the correct answer?
2. What roles did the team members play?

Variation
1. The problem may be made more difficult by including other irrelevant information.

Source
Adapted from 'Room 703: Information Sharing', J. William Pfeiffer and John E. Jones, *A Handbook of Structured Experiences for Human Relations Training*, Volume 5, University Associates, California, 1975.

Solution

Room	Period			
	1	2	3	4
700	Ms Jones	Mr Lee	Ms Martin	Mr Jacobs
701	Mr Jacobs	Ms Martin	Mr Lee	Ms Jones
702	Ms Martin	Ms Jones	Mr Jacobs	Mr Lee
703	MR LEE	MR JACOBS	MS JONES	MS MARTIN

Room 703 Information Cards

You may tell your group what is on this card, but do not pass it around for others to read.

Information
- Room 701 has Mr Lee for teaching during the third period.
- Ms Jones and Ms Carr do not get along well, so they do not work together.
- During the first period, the team leader, whom Harry likes, teaches Room 702.

You may tell your group what is on this card, but do not pass it around for others to read..

Information
- All teachers teach at the same time and exchange groups at the end of each period.
- Each teacher likes a different group best. During the second period, each teacher teaches the group they like best.
- Each teacher teaches each group during one of the first four periods of the day.

You may tell your group what is on this card, but do not pass it around for others to read...

Information
- The school has two teachers' aides, four teachers, and four groups of students.
- Ms Martin is the team leader for the English Unit.
- Mr Lee likes to work with Room 700.
- Ms Jones teaches Room 701 during the fourth period but likes Room 702 best.

You may tell your group what is on this card, but do not pass it around for others to read....

Information
- Your group members have all the information needed to find the answer to the following question. In what sequence are the teachers (by name) in Room 703 during the first four periods?
- Only one answer is correct and you can prove it.
- You are to present the group's findings in no longer than 20 minutes.

You may tell your group what is on this card, but do not pass it around for others to read.....

Information
- Ms Carr and Mr Jacobs disagree about how it would be best to handle Room 702, in which there seems to be a history of abusing substitute teachers.
- The team leader has been at this school for five years.
- Ms Carr has been at this school longer than anyone else.

You may tell your group what is on this card, but do not pass it around for others to read......

Information
- The team leader teaches Room 701 during the second period.
- Harry works with Room 702 during the second period.
- Ms Martin has been at this school for the shortest period of time.

---

59. **List of Names**

Overview
This is an exercise that can be used with an established group. The exercise has the potential of letting participants see how others in the group see them.

Goal
1. To allow participants the opportunity to see how others in the group perceive them.

Time required
Depends on application.

Size of group
Unlimited.

Material required
A prepared list of participant names, cut into strips.

Procedure
1. Inform the group members that they are going to be involved in a role reversal. They are going to be given another person's name from the group and then they are to act out their perceptions of that person.

2. Pass around an envelope with the list of names inside it so participants can each select a name at random and keep it to themselves. During the day they are to act out that person's role. This can either be done at an identified time or randomly during the activities. Tell participants that this is meant to be fun and that they are not to be destructive about another person's characteristics.

Note: It is very important that this exercise be thoroughly debriefed to eliminate negative feelings.

Discussion points
1. Was everyone able to identify who had whose name? Why?
2. Are some of these perceptions incorrect?
3. What can we do about bad/unwanted traits?
4. Does anyone want to comment on the performance of the person acting out their role?

Variations
1. The slips can be selected during one day's activities and the participants told that they are to act out the role for the whole of the next day.
2. You may want to select who gets certain names.

Trainer's notes

Overview

This exercise shows participants how directions are interpreted differently by different people.

Goals

1. To allow participants to see how instructions/directions are interpreted in different ways by different people.
2. To get participants thinking about ways in which they can improve their communication skills.

Time required

10 minutes.

Size of group

Unlimited.

Material required

A sheet of A4 paper for each participant.

Procedure

1. Give each participant a sheet of A4 paper. Then ask them to close their eyes and follow your directions. Tell them that they are not to ask any questions during the instructional phase.

2. Give the following directions. Firstly, fold the sheet in half. Then fold it in half again. Then fold it in half yet again. Tear the right-hand corner off. Turn the sheet over and tear the left-hand corner off.

3. Now get the group to open their eyes and unfold their sheets of paper. It should be immediately obvious that all of the group do not have the same finished product.

4. This now leads into a discussion on how to improve communication skills.

Discussion points

1. Why didn't everyone finish up with the same end product?
2. Were the instructions easy to follow? Why? Why not?
3. Why do we need to improve our instructional skills?
4. How could the instructions be improved?

Variations

1. More directions can be given for the folding and tearing.
2. Get one of the participants to give the instructions.

Trainer's notes

61. Learning By Linking   ICMLS

Overview
This exercise shows how recall is made easier by the use of association.

Goal
1. To show participants how association makes recall easier.

Time required
5–10 minutes.

Size of group
Unlimited.

Material required
A pen for each participant and sufficient copies of Lists A and B.

Procedure
1. Explain that recall can be made easier. Then mentally divide the group into 2 subgroups.
2. Give all participants in half of the group a copy of 'List A' face down. Give the participants in the other half of the group a copy of 'List B'. Ask them not to look at the list until they are told to do so.
3. Tell the participants that they will be given 2 minutes to study the list they have and that they should try to remember as many words from the list as possible. Now tell them to turn their lists over.
4. After the 2 minutes have elapsed ask them to turn their lists face down again and write as many

words from the list as they can remember. They have another 2 minutes for this phase.
5. When the time is up ask them to total the number of correct words that they have been able to recall, including any headings written down. Get the totals from the individuals and place them somewhere visible, heading the scores 'List A' and 'List B'.
6. It will become very obvious that 'List B' has much higher scores than 'List A'. Point out that the 2 lists contain the same 60 words. Ask the participants to exchange lists with each other so that they may see what was different with the 2 lists.

Discussion points
1. Why was it easier to recall more information from 'List B'?
2. Tasks as well as lists may be broken into much more digestible chunks, rather than having too many disjointed pieces of information.

Variation
1. Words and groupings may be rewritten to suit the organisation.

Source
Adapted from the Programme Development Module: Basic Methods of Instruction course, conducted by Training and Development Services, University of Technology, Sydney.

Trainer's notes

List A

DOG	GAS	PANTS
ANIMALS	SILK	COAL
OIL	COTTON	CAT
TABLE	CLOTH	FUELS
WOOL	BASEBALL	HAMMER
COW	KNIFE	BASKETBALL
FRUIT	TENNIS	BOMB
PAN	CHAIR	YELLOW
GREEN	COLOUR	PROFESSION
SOFA	SCREWDRIVER	DENTIST
DOCTOR	SHOES	FOOTBALL
FURNITURE	TEACHER	RIFLE
HORSE	BLUE	APPLE
RAYON	UTENSILS	SPORT
SAW	ORANGE	WEAPONS
WOOD	TOOLS	CLOTHING
NAILS	SPOON	LAWYER
GUN	SHIRT	PEAR
SOCKS	FORK	BANANA
RED	BED	DAGGER

List B

ANIMALS	**CLOTHS**	**FUELS**
DOG	COTTON	OIL
CAT	WOOL	GAS
HORSE	SILK	COAL
COW	RAYON	WOOD

FRUITS	**COLOURS**	**PROFESSIONS**
APPLE	BLUE	DOCTOR
ORANGE	RED	LAWYER
PEAR	GREEN	TEACHER
BANANA	YELLOW	DENTIST

FURNITURE	**UTENSILS**	**SPORTS**
CHAIR	KNIFE	FOOTBALL
TABLE	SPOON	BASEBALL
BED	FORK	BASKETBALL
SOFA	PAN	TENNIS

WEAPONS	**TOOLS**	**CLOTHING**
DAGGER	HAMMER	SHIRTS
GUN	SAW	SOCKS
RIFLE	NAILS	PANTS
BOMB	SCREWDRIVER	SHOES

Overview
This quick exercise shows participants that they need to give an overall picture with an instruction or description.

Goal
1. To show that an instruction or description needs to be put into context.

Time required
5 minutes.

Size of group
Unlimited.

Material required
Sufficient copies of 'The Procedure' handout.

Procedure
1. Tell the group that they are going to be given a very clear procedural description. They will have 2 minutes to read the handout.
2. Give all of the participants a copy of 'The Procedure' handout. They should also be told that if they recognise the description they are to raise their hand without telling the others what it is.

3. After the 2 minutes are up, tell the group that even very clear instructions or descriptions need to be put into context. Then ask the group if the words 'clothes' and 'washing' were added, could the handout now be followed.

Discussion points
1. Do we give instructions like this back in the workplace?
2. Do we always have to put our instructions and descriptions into context?

Variations
1. Any other procedure could be used as long as the facilitator ensures the participants will not recognise the description.
2. Teams could be formed with a prize for the first group to work out what the procedure is.

Source
Adapted from the Programme Development Module: Basic Methods of Instruction course, conducted by Training and Development Services, University of Technology, Sydney.

Trainer's notes

The Procedure

The procedure is actually quite simple. First you arrange things into different groups. Of course, one pile may be sufficient depending on how much there is to do. If you have to go somewhere else due to lack of facilities that is the next step, otherwise you are pretty well set. It is important not to overdo things. That is, it is better to do too few things at once than too many. In the short run this may not seem important but complications can easily arise. A mistake can be expensive as well. At first the whole procedure will seem complicated. Soon, however, it will become just another facet of life. It is difficult to foresee any end to the necessity for this task in the immediate future, but then one can never tell. After the procedure is completed one arranges the materials into different groups again. Then they can be put into their appropriate places. Eventually they will be used once more and the whole cycle will have to be repeated. However, this is part of life.

Overview
This is an exercise showing participants how to identify sources of stress.

Goal
1. To identify sources of stress.

Time required
15 minutes.

Size of group
Unlimited.

Material required
A pen and paper for each participant and a prepared 'Circuit Board' chart for the facilitator to display.

Procedure
1. Start the discussion on what are the main sources of stress for the individual.
2. Give each participant a pen and paper. Ask them to take 3 or 4 minutes to write down their main sources of stress.
3. After the time has elapsed, display the prepared 'Circuit Board' and ask each participant to reveal one of their sources of stress. As these are identified, place them in one of the blank spaces on the diagram.
4. When the diagram is full, tell the participants that they are similar to this circuit board. A circuit board may overload (breakdown) if it is required to handle too much. In the same way we may overload (breakdown) if we are required to handle too much.
5. Then lead the discussion into stress management techniques.

Discussion points
1. Are we similar to the circuit board?
2. Did anyone feel stressed by this exercise? Why?
3. What techniques do we use to avoid overload?

Variation
1. Can be done in small groups of 5–7 participants.

Source
Adapted from 'Circuit Overload', Nancy Loving Tubesing and Donald A. Tubesing, *Structured Exercises in Stress Management*, Volume 2, Whole Person Press, Duluth MN, 1983.

Trainer's notes

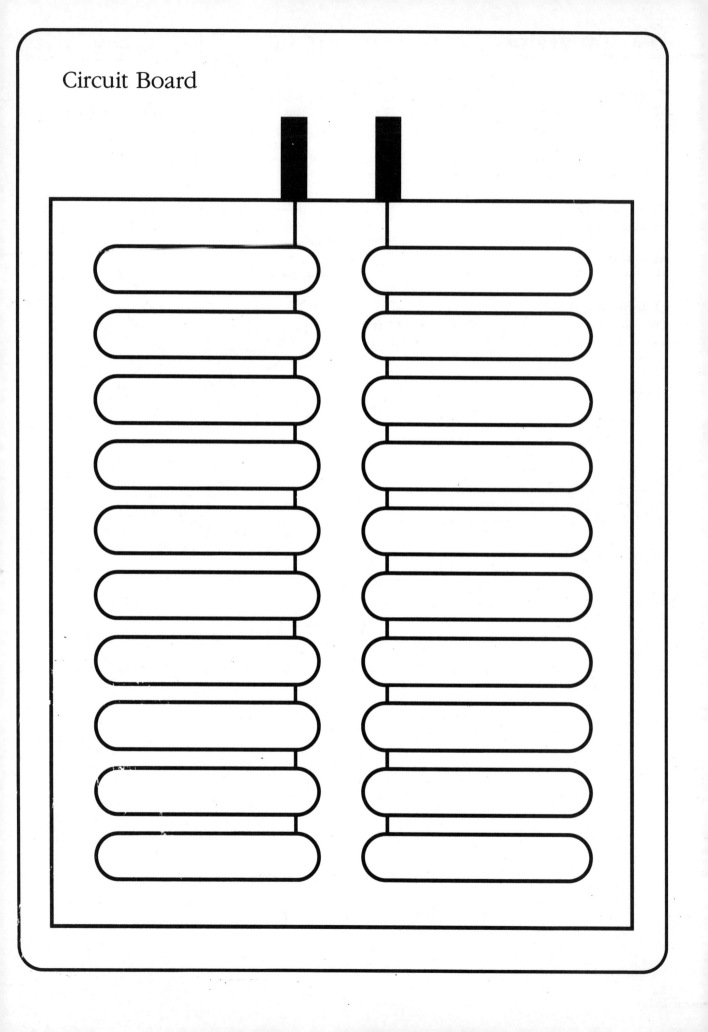

Circuit Board

64. Tangrams

Overview
This is a Chinese silhouette puzzle.

Goals
1. To solve the puzzles.
2. To get participants working together.

Time required
15–20 minutes.

Size of group
Unlimited.

Material required
One set of tans (shapes as silhouettes) cut from cardboard for each team and a set of prepared diagrams for posting or projecting.

Procedure
1. Introduce tangrams. Tangrams are a Chinese puzzle. They are similar to a jigsaw puzzle but they use tans instead of pieces of a picture.
2. Divide the group into teams of 5–7 participants. Give each team a set of tans.
3. Show the first complete silhouette and ask the teams to sing out when they have the solution. Repeat the process for all 5 silhouettes.

Discussion points
1. Did anyone notice that this is different to a jigsaw puzzle in that there is more than one solution?
2. Is this type of puzzle more realistic to the workplace as we nearly always have the solutions, but sometimes we have to adapt them to make them work.

Variations
1. This can be done individually rather than in teams.
2. Prizes can be awarded for each team first with the solution.
3. Time limits can be applied.

Source
Adapted from *Tangrams*, Ronald C. Read, Dover Publishing Inc., New York, 1965.

Solution

Trainer's notes

Tangrams

Below is the template for making your own set of cardboard tans.
One set is required for each team.

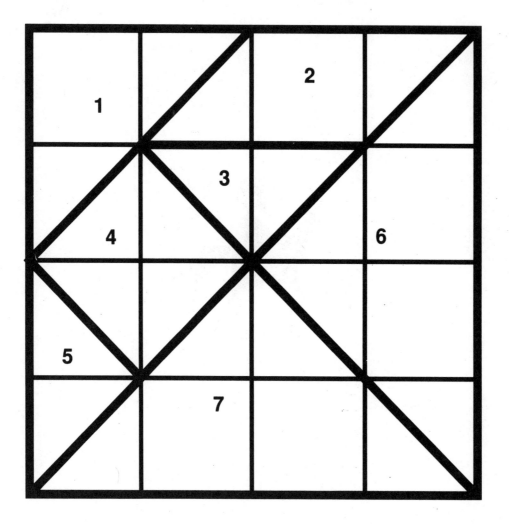

Tangrams

65. In-Tray

Overview
This exercise shows participants how to use correct self-management techniques.

Goals
1. To get participants thinking about priorities.
2. To allow participants to practise time management principles.

Time required
20–30 minutes.

Size of group
Up to 18.

Material required
An in-tray and a full set of documents (mail) for each team. Each team will require a work area.

Prepare all mail items well before training commences. The items should be relevant to the group's workplace and duties. Aim for about 20–30 items for the tray, and about another 10–15 for the second mail drop. The items should be a mixture of routine items, urgent matters, important matters, trivial matters, junk mail, magazines, articles and one very urgent and important item placed towards the bottom of the pile.

Procedure
1. Begin by introducing time management and self-management principles.

2. Break the group into teams of 3 or 4 participants. Give each team an in-tray with a full set of documents to handle. A time limit of 10 minutes is set to complete the in-tray.
3. During the exercise, place additional 'mail' in each in-tray.
4. After the 10 minutes has passed, get each team to present the large group with the priority they placed on each piece of mail and what they did with each item. Also ask them to give reasons for their decisions.

Discussion points
1. Did everyone come up with the same basic results?
2. How did people feel when the second mail drop arrived?
3. Were good time management and/or self-management techniques used?

Variations
1. This exercise can be done individually rather than in teams.
2. The second mail drop may be left out.
3. The facilitator can interrupt and disturb the teams as they are trying to sort their mail out.

Trainer's notes

Overview
This will show why learning should be a paced process, rather than a short intense experience.

Goal
1. To show participants that time is required for better or more efficient learning to take place.

Time required
15–20 minutes.

Size of group
Unlimited.

Material required
A pen and a sheet of paper for each participant. A stopwatch for the facilitator and somewhere to display the results.

Procedure
1. Lead the discussion about distributed practice (explaining leaving rest periods between practice sessions), and the fact that it is better to learn little bits often as opposed to large sections at a time.
2. Break the large group into 2 groups (a control group and an experimental group). Take one group out of the room and give members something else to do.
3. Give the members of the group remaining in the room a pen and paper. Read them the instructions from the 'Distributed Practice Information Sheet'. No discussion is allowed.
4. Then get this half of the group to carry out their assigned task with the 30-second extra rest between trials.
5. On completion the 2 groups swap over. With the second half of the group (the control group) again read out the instructions from the 'Distributed Practice Information Sheet'.
6. Then get this half of the group to carry out their assigned tasks without the 30-second extra rest between trials.
7. When completed, bring both groups back together. Ask the participants to count the total number of correct letters for each trial. Tally the scores, average them between groups and display them. Then resume the discussion on distributed practice.

Discussion point
1. Which type of practice led to faster learning with this particular task?

Variations
1. Numbers may be used in place of letters.
2. Observers and scorers may be used during the whole exercise.

Trainer's notes

Distributed practice information sheet

During this session you will be asked to print the letters of the alphabet upside down and from right to left but in their correct order. This means that when you turn your sheet around, the letters will appear as if you had written them up the right way. You are to concentrate primarily on speed. Your score depends on how many letters you print correctly. If you make a mistake, simply print over it and continue printing.

When you are told to begin, start printing from the right-hand side to the left-hand side of the paper. Start on the top line and print the alphabet upside down in alphabetical order. Each time you complete the alphabet, begin the alphabet again from that point on the page, until your time is finished. Do not stop at the end of the alphabet unless your time has run out. Simply start again with the letter A and continue. Each trial lasts 30 seconds. Be sure to cover previous trials with a blank sheet of paper so that you cannot see what has been written before. At the end of each 30-second trial, you will have 10 seconds to turn your work around and look for mistakes. If you are learning with distributed practice, you will have an additional 30-second rest between trials.

Overview
This is a quick exercise to test the individual's memory and then to see how much better the results are using synergy.

Goals
1. To allow the participants to see synergy working.
2. To look at a decision-making process.

Time required
30–40 minutes.

Size of group
Unlimited.

Material required
A pen and a copy of 'The Questions' for each participant.

Procedure
1. Introduce the decision-making exercise and the term 'synergy'.
2. Read out the story to the group. Then give the participants a copy of 'The Questions' and instruct them to take 5 minutes to answer all of the questions on the sheet. Then ask them to form groups of 5–7 members.
3. When the groups are formed, ask them to answer 'The Questions' again, but this time they are to discuss the responses among themselves. They should be allowed about 10 minutes to complete this phase.
4. Then give the participants the correct answers and

ask them to compare the individual results with the group results.
5. Then direct the discussion back to the decision-making process and synergy.

Discussion points
1. Did the group answers score better than the individual answers?
2. Did any individual have a better score than the group? What relevance should we place on this?
3. Can this process be used in the workplace or at home?

Variation
1. The story can be written to suit the participants' or organisation's needs.

The story
Margaret was driving along Elizabeth Street early in the morning when she noticed 2 people walk quickly out of a service station. She had to stop for a red light. While she was stopped she saw the 2 people get into a small European car and take off very quickly. The car was silver in colour and its registration was COOL 1. As they drove away, a man came racing out of the service station shouting and waving his arms. She drove over to the man and found that he had just been robbed. The stolen items included over $400 in cash, 15 cartons of cigarettes and the man's wallet. When the police arrived a few minutes later they gave her this list of questions to answer. Can you answer them for her?

Trainer's notes

The Questions

1. What is the witness's name?

2. Where were you when you saw this event?

3. What time did this happen?

4. How many people were there, and what sex were they?

5. Can you describe them?

6. Who was robbed? (Include their position and description if possible.)

7. Did this person run out of the office?

8. Can you describe the vehicle they drove away in?

9. What was stolen?

10. Who had a weapon?

68. Tennis Balls

Overview
This is a quick exercise to get participants thinking.

Goals
1. To energise the group.
2. To get participants thinking.
3. To see who takes which team role.

Time required
5–10 minutes.

Size of group
Unlimited.

Material required
Sufficient pens and copies of 'The Tennis Court'.

Procedure
1. Tell the group members that they are going to participate in a problem-solving activity.
2. Break the group into teams of 5–7 members. Tell them that they will be given a handout showing a view looking down on a tennis court. The tennis court will have 15 tennis balls lying on it. Each team's task is to divide the court into 5 sections with each section containing 3 balls. They are only allowed to use 3 straight lines to divide the court.
3. Now give the teams a copy of 'The Tennis Court' handout. When all groups have finished conclude the exercise and move into the discussion.

4. At the conclusion start a discussion on team members' roles if appropriate.

Discussion points
1. Which team arrived at a solution first?
2. Which team members took charge, etc.?

Variations
1. This may be done on an individual basis.
2. A time limit may be imposed.

Solution

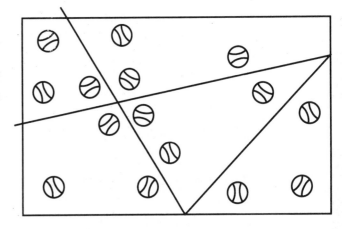

Trainer's notes

The Tennis Court

Overview

This encourages participants to plan some fun into their daily activities.

Goals

1. To get all participants to plan a fun activity into each day over the next month.
2. To allow participants to see that even fun activities must be planned for or they may miss out.

Time required

30 minutes.

Size of group

Unlimited.

Material required

A copy of the 'Fun Activities Sheet' and a pen for each person.

Procedure

1. Introduce the exercise by saying that even fun or childish activities need to be planned into your schedule otherwise they may be forgotten or overlooked. If they are forgotten or overlooked this may affect performance due to increased stress levels. People need to let off steam occasionally.

2. Give each participant a pen and a copy of the 'Fun Activities Sheet'. They are now told that they have 15 minutes to plan one fun activity for each day over the next month. Some examples of fun activities can be given, such as going for a jog, surfing, playing marbles with the kids, going for a walk around the block, playing a practical joke, etc. Also tell them that it is okay to use the same activity as long as it doesn't become too repetitive. They should try to use their imagination.

3. At the conclusion the group members should quickly share their planned activities with each other.

Discussion points

1. Did everyone complete the task?
2. After members saw each other's activities did they feel that they wanted to alter theirs? (If they do you can give them another few minutes to modify their sheets.)
3. Who plans these types of activities into their diaries now?
4. Do you think it would be a good idea to include them in your diary?

Variations

1. This may be done in small groups.
2. Have someone judge the best set of activities.

Trainer's notes

Fun Activities Sheet

Sunday	Monday	Tuesday	Wednesday	Thursday	Friday	Saturday

70. My Worries

Overview
This is a possible way for participants to ensure they give the facilitator their full attention.

Goal
1. To allow participants to identify any worries and concerns they have before the session starts.

Time required
10 minutes.

Size of group
Unlimited.

Material required
A copy of the 'My Worries' sheet and a pen for each participant.

Procedure
1. Inform the group that they will be required to devote their full attention to the session commencing shortly. Tell them that there is a way to ensure that their worries and concerns don't interfere with the process.
2. Give each participant a pen and a copy of the 'My Worries' sheet and ask them to take 5 minutes to write down all of their immediate worries and concerns. Let them know that this sheet will not be seen by anyone else.
3. When they have completed their lists, ask them to fold the sheets up (or tear them up) and throw them into the bin provided.
4. Now that they have thrown their worries and concerns away they will be able to give you their full attention. You can also tell them that their worries and concerns may not be as serious at the end of the session as they were at the beginning.

Discussion points
1. Does anyone have anything else they would like to get rid of?
2. What sometimes happens to problems when we put them out of our mind for a while?

Variation
1. Get participants to place the 'My Worries' sheets in envelopes and seal them. Get them to write their name on the envelopes and give them to you. Tell the group that you will hold their worries and concerns until the end of the session, then they will be handed back to them.

Trainer's notes

My worries
and concerns are ...

Overview

This exercise allows team discussion and problem-solving activities.

Goals

1. To allow participants to tackle a problem-solving activity.
2. To allow participants to see how important communication is in this type of activity.
3. To let the group see how synergy creates a better solution for the majority of the people involved in the decision-making process.

Time required

45–60 minutes.

Size of group

Unlimited.

Material required

A copy of the 'Moon Explorer Problem' and a pen for each individual.

Procedure

1. Read out the 'Moon Explorer Problem'.
2. Give a copy of the 'Moon Explorer Problem' and a pen to each individual. Tell the participants that they are to rank the 15 items in the order of priority that they would choose. They are not to discuss the problem with anyone else at this stage. Allow them 5 minutes to make their decisions.
3. Then break the group into teams of 5–7 participants. Tell each team that it is to discuss the individual rankings and to come up with a group consensus ranking. The rules are as follows.
   - Everyone in the team must agree with the choice.
   - No voting or compromising is allowed.
   - The final decision must be acceptable to everyone and a decision must be reached within 20 minutes.

- The leader of the group must be able to give reasons for the inclusion and exclusion of the various items.
4. After the time has expired each team reports back to the large group with its findings.
5. Then you compare the individual results with the team results and then with the 'Experts' Rankings'. Then point out to the group what synergy has done to create a better solution for the majority of the group.

Discussion points

1. Who got a better result by themselves?
2. What does synergy do for us?
3. How can we use synergy to our advantage?

Source

Detailed simulations similar to this are produced by Human Synergistics, 39819 Plymouth Road, Plymouth, Michigan 48170 USA.

Experts' rankings

A.	box of matches	13
B.	food concentrate	4
C.	20 metres of nylon rope	6
D.	parachute silk	3
E.	portable heating unit	15
F.	two .45 calibre pistols	9
G.	one case dehydrated pet milk	11
H.	two 50 kilogram tanks of oxygen	1
I.	stellar map (as seen from the moon)	5
J.	life jacket	10
K.	magnetic compass	14
L.	20 litres of water	2
M.	signal flares	12
N.	first aid kit and needles	8
O.	solar powered FM receiver transmitter	7

Trainer's notes

Moon Explorer Problem

Instructions

You are a space crew originally scheduled to rendezvous with a mother ship on the lighted surface of the moon. Due to mechanical difficulties, however, your ship was forced to land at a spot some 300 kilometres from the rendezvous point. During re-entry and landing, much of the equipment aboard was damaged. Since survival depends on reaching the mother ship, the most critical items available must be chosen for the 300 kilometre trip. Below are listed the 15 items left intact and undamaged after landing. Your task is to reach the rendezvous point. Place the number 1 by the most important item, the number 2 by the second most important item, and so on through to number 15, the least important. Please ensure that you don't change your indivdual answers during the following group discussion.

	Individual ranking	Group consensus
A. box of matches	____	____
B. food concentrate	____	____
C. 20 metres of nylon rope	____	____
D. parachute silk	____	____
E. portable heating unit	____	____
F. two .45 calibre pistols	____	____
G. one case dehydrated pet milk	____	____
H. two 50 kilogram tanks of oxygen	____	____
I. stellar map (as seen from the moon)	____	____
J. life jacket	____	____
K. magnetic compass	____	____
L. 20 litres of water	____	____
M. signal flares	____	____
N. first aid kit and needles	____	____
O. solar powered FM receiver transmitter	____	____

Overview
This exercise allows team discussion and problem-solving activities. It may also be used for equal employment opportunity issues, discrimination issues and stereotyping.

Goals
1. To allow participants to tackle a problem-solving activity.
2. To allow participants to see how important communication is in this type of activity.
3. To let the group see how synergy creates a better solution for the majority of the people involved in the decision-making process.
4. To allow participants to experience stereotyping problems, equal employment opportunity issues and discrimination issues.

Time required
45–60 minutes.

Size of group
Unlimited.

Material required
A copy of the 'Fall-out Shelter Problem' and a pen for each individual.

Procedure
1. Read out the 'Fall-out Shelter Problem'.
2. Hand out a copy of the 'Fall-out Shelter Problem' and a pen to each individual. Tell the participants that they are to select 6 of the 12 people to remain in the shelter. They are not to discuss the problem with anyone else at this stage. They are allowed 5 minutes to make their decisions.
3. Then break the group into teams of 5–7 participants. Tell each team that it is to discuss the individual rankings and to come up with a group consensus ranking. The rules are as follows.
   • Everyone in the team must agree with the choice.
   • No voting or compromising is allowed.
   • The final decision must be acceptable to everyone and a decision must be reached within 20 minutes.
   • The leader of the group must be able to give reasons for the inclusion and exclusion of the various people.
4. After the time has expired each team reports back to the large group with its findings.
5. Compare the individual results with the team results. Point out to the group what synergy has done to create a better solution for the majority of the group. You must debrief this exercise completely as some equal employment opportunity and stereotyping issues will be raised.

Discussion points
1. How did people like having the power of life or death?
2. Do we tend to stereotype different groups?
3. What does synergy do for us?
4. How can we use synergy to our advantage?

Source
Detailed simulations similar to this are produced by Human Synergistics, 39819 Plymouth Road, Plymouth, Michigan 48170 USA.

Trainer's notes

Fall-out Shelter Problem

Situation

You are a civil defence committee appointed by the Prime Minister to make decisions on fall-out shelter occupancy. War has been declared. It appears that only the occupants of a fall-out shelter in central Australia have a good chance for survival. The civil defence director has informed Canberra that at present 12 people are occupying the shelter. The computers have calculated that the shelter can guarantee survival for only 6 people. Your committee is to decide which 6 are to be excluded from the group: 6 must go and the remaining 6 may live to rebuild a complete new society. Please ensure that you don't change your individual answers during the following group discussion.

		Individual selection	Group consensus
1.	36-year-old female physician, known to be a racist	____	____
2.	army drill instructor	____	____
3.	black militant, biological researcher	____	____
4.	biochemist	____	____
5.	olympic athlete, all sports	____	____
6.	film starlet	____	____
7.	third year medical student, homosexual	____	____
8.	16-year-old girl of questionable IQ, pregnant	____	____
9.	30-year-old Catholic priest	____	____
10.	38-year-old male carpenter, 'Mr Fix-it' man, served 7 years for drug offences, has been out of gaol for 3 months	____	____
11.	22-year-old army nurse and midwife, homosexual	____	____
12.	15-year-old boy, first-year apprentice carpenter	____	____

Overview
This is a quick exercise to show how many participants stereotype roles.

Goals
1. To make participants aware of stereotyping.
2. To keep participants busy while waiting for others to arrive.

Time required
10–15 minutes.

Size of group
Unlimited.

Material required
A pen and paper for each participant.

Procedure
1. Introduce the exercise without indicating anything at all about stereotyping.
2. Give the participants a pen and paper. Read out 'A Case of Labelling'. Ask them to note their answers on the piece of paper, without the benefit of discussion.
3. Post each participant's response on the board. On completion of the exercise it will probably be necessary to highlight the follies of labelling or stereotyping.

Trainer's notes

Discussion points
1. Why do we stereotype people or put labels on them?
2. Do we stereotype people in the workplace?
3. How can we avoid stereotyping or labelling?

Variation
1. Other one-sex-dominated professions may be used.

Solution
The boy's mother.

A case of labelling
A father and son decided to go for a drive one Sunday morning.

Unfortunately, both were involved in a very serious car accident.

Two ambulances arrived. The father, on being placed in the ambulance, died.

The son was critically injured and rushed to emergency for an immediate operation.

The surgeon, on entering the theatre, saw the boy and said, 'I can't operate on that boy, he's my son'.

What relationship was the surgeon to the boy?

74. Faces

Overview
The exercise could be used at the start and at the conclusion of training to determine participants' feelings.

Goals
1. To allow the participants to reveal their feelings at the beginning and at the end of training.
2. To allow the facilitator to debrief undesired feelings at the end of training rather than have those feelings taken back to the workplace.

Time required
20–30 minutes at the start of training and 20–30 minutes at the conclusion of training. These times may vary considerably depending on the length of training and the indicated feelings.

Size of group
Unlimited.

Material required
Sufficient copies of the 'How Do You Feel Today?' sheet and a pen for each participant.

Procedure
1. After welcoming the participants, hand out pens and copies of the 'How Do You Feel Today?' sheet and ask the group to indicate their feelings as they feel now.
2. When the sheets are completed, ask each participant to reveal their responses to the group. This allows you and the group to rectify any negative feelings or attitudes now rather than have the problem later on. After the discussion start the program.
3. At the conclusion of the program, again hand out pens and copies of the 'How Do You Feel Today?' sheet. Ask participants to indicate their feelings.
4. Then debrief the feelings and attitudes indicated by the participants.

Discussion points
1. Do these feelings interfere with our learning and application?
2. Do we generally tend to hide these feelings?
3. Did anyone feel threatened by this exposure?

Variation
1. For longer training sessions the activity may be used a number of times.

Source
Heather Waugh, Sydney, NSW.

Trainer's notes

How Do You Feel Today? (Please indicate which faces apply)

Aggressive   Anxious   Apologetic   Arrogant   Bashful

Blissful   Bored   Cautious   Cold   Confident

Curious   Determined   Disappointed   Disbelieving   Enraged

Envious   Exhausted   Frightened   Frustrated   Guilty

Happy   Horrified   Hot   Hungover   Hurt

Hysterical   Indifferent   Interested   Jealous   Lonely

Lovestruck   Negative   Regretful   Relieved   Sad

Satisfied   Surprised   Suspicious   Undecided   Other …

75. Follow-up to Murphy's Law

Overview
This is a quick exercise that can be used when things are going wrong for the facilitator.

Goals
1. To give the participants a little light-hearted relief.
2. To give the facilitator a little breathing time and a chance to regroup his or her thoughts.

Time required
5–10 minutes

Size of group
Unlimited.

Material required
A copy of the 'Follow-up to Murphy's Law' information sheet.

Procedure
1. When things are going wrong for the facilitator, he or she should stop the presentation and read out

'Follow-up to Murphy's Law'. Explain that Murphy's Law (Whatever can go wrong, will) is attributed to an air force captain who apparently created the now-famous phrase when a series of errors and problems kept occurring in a Californian air force base missile site. The follow-up items are things which most people can relate to.
2. Some form of quick discussion may be appropriate afterwards.

Discussion point
1. Can anyone add any other follow up items that may have been overlooked?

Source
Adapted from Laurence J. Peter, author of *The Peter Principle*, and from 'Beyond Murphy', Edward E. Scannell and John W. Newstrom, *More Games Trainers Play*, McGraw-Hill, Inc., New York, 1983.

Trainer's notes

Follow-up to Murphy's Law

Murphy's Law is attributed to an air force captain who apparently created the now-famous phrase when a series of errors and problems kept occurring in a Californian air force base missile site. These are some of follow-up items to which most people can relate.

1. Left to themselves, things tend to go from bad to worse.
2. Whenever you set out to do something, something else must be done first.
3. Nothing is as easy as it looks.
4. Everything takes longer than you think.
5. If there is the possibility of several things going wrong, the one that will cause the most damage will be the one.
6. Nature always sides with the hidden flaw.
7. It always costs more than first estimated.
8. It is easier to get involved in something than it is to get out of it.
9. Every solution breeds new problems.
10. If you try to please everybody, somebody will be disappointed.
11. It is impossible to make anything foolproof, because fools are so clever.
12. If you tinker with anything long enough, it will break.
13. By making things absolutely clear, people will become confused.
14. If there is a 50 per cent chance of success, that means there is a 75 per cent chance of failure.
15. Interchangeable parts won't.
16. In any computation, the figure that is obviously correct will be the source of error.
17. Blame will never be placed if enough people are involved.
18. Nothing is lost until you begin looking for it.
19. If in the course of several months only three worthwhile social events take place, they will all fall on the same evening.
20. Murphy was an optimist!

76. Them and Us

Overview
This is an exercise to show how we feel about being left out.

Goal
1. To show participants how minority groups may feel.

Time required
5 minutes before a break and 15–60 minutes after the break.

Size of group
Unlimited, but if more than 24 it becomes difficult to debrief all participants.

Material required
A sufficient number of prepared name tags and information sheets for the whole group and a rather elaborate morning tea. One end of the room should be set up with tables, tablecloths, comfortable chairs, china cups and saucers, spoons, tea pots, quantities of cream biscuits, quantities of cakes, etc. This end of the room must be marked for the 'Us' group. The other end of the room should be set up with a single table, a hot water supply, disposable cups and stirrers, coffee sachets, tea bags, and a packet of dry biscuits. Make certain that there are no chairs, tablecloths, sugar or milk. This end of the room must be marked for the 'Them' group.

Procedure
1. Indicate that there is going to be a coffee break in 5 minutes. Before anyone is allowed to leave the room give them a name tag to wear during the break. Half of the name tags will read 'Them' and the other half will read 'Us'.
2. Tell participants that during the break the 'Them' group will be served at one end of the room and the 'Us' group will be served at the other end of the room. Now ask them to read (but not discuss or divulge) the information supplied to them with their name tags.
3. The group now has the morning tea break. Ask participants again to follow their instructions.
4. After the break bring the group back and thoroughly debrief the exercise. It is important to include all participants in the debrief as some people can feel some powerful, and even hostile, feelings from this exercise.

Discussion points
1. How did people feel during the break?
2. What did members of one group think the other group thought?
3. Who broke the rules? Why?
4. How can we improve this type of situation?

Variations
1. 'Them' and 'Us' labels may be replaced with more appropriate titles such as 'Management' and 'Workers', etc.
2. Some of the group can be used as observers.

Source
Adapted from 'Them and Us', Elizabeth M. Christopher and Larry E. Smith, *Leadership Training Through Gaming,* Nichols Publishing Co., New York, and Kogan Page Limited, London, 1987.

Trainer's notes

Information sheet for the 'Them' group

During the coffee break you will all find yourselves to be members of either an 'in-group' or an 'out-group'. Unfortunately, you are one of the 'out-group', which is shown by your name tag, which says 'Them'. You may not take your refreshments from the table near the chairs—your table is the one in the corner at the other end. The chairs are reserved for the use of those whose name tags read 'Us'. You may sit on the floor if you wish. If you need anything from the 'Us' table, you may go over and ask for it, but be sure that your manner is respectful and that you show by your behaviour that you understand the exalted status of the 'Us' people. If by any chance an 'Us' person approaches your table, this is a great honour which you should acknowledge appropriately.

Information sheet for the 'Us' group

During the following coffee break you will all find yourself to be members of an 'in-group' or an 'out-group'. You are fortunate to be a member of the 'in-group', which means that you are one of 'Us', not 'Them'. You will recognise the others who share your exalted status by the 'Us' name tags that they wear. Please join them at the senior managers' table and sit in the comfortable chairs. If any of 'Them' approach your table with a request of any kind, you will, of course, make sure that they behave respectfully or you will send them away. Please enjoy your refreshments and the company of the select 'Us' group.

77. The Brainstorm

Overview
This is a brainstorming exercise that allows selected participants to use real problems.

Goals
1. To allow participants to see how effective brainstorming is.
2. To allow participants to see the benefit of brainstorming in a problem-solving situation.

Time required
60–90 minutes.

Size of group
Unlimited, but broken into subgroups of 5–7 participants.

Material required
Butcher's paper and markers for each subgroup.

Procedure
1. Ask the participants to form subgroups of 5–7 people.
2. Call for a volunteer from each subgroup. Volunteers must have a problem they would like solved. Take the volunteers outside the room and ask them to divulge the problem they would like solved. This is to ensure that the problem is suitable for this exercise and not too sensitive or difficult.
3. Tell the subgroups that they are going to be given a problem to quickly think about and come up with solutions. Also tell them that the person posing the problem will be writing down their ideas one at a time. They are not allowed to discuss or criticise any of the suggestions during the brainstorming phase, which will last 5–10 minutes.
4. Ask the volunteers to rejoin their subgroups and tell them their problem. The volunteers write down the suggested solutions.
5. After the brainstorming phase, the individual subgroups may then discuss the solutions one at a time and get clarification from the person making the suggestion if needed. The subgroup is then asked to come up with the best 2 or 3 solutions as identified from the brainstorming phase.
6. All the subgroups go back to the main group with their solutions. Ask the main group to identify and discuss the best 2 or 3 solutions overall.
7. The exercise is debriefed, pointing out that the solutions the subgroups offered would have totalled far more in number than would have been generated by the individuals alone.

Discussion points
1. Did the person posing the problem get any possible solutions?
2. Did anyone find it hard not to talk about each suggestion as it came up?
3. Can people see an application for this type of problem-solving process back in the workplace?

Variations
1. You may pose the same problem to each subgroup.
2. Problems can be swapped around between subgroups for a solution, and then be reported back to the person posing the problem.

Trainer's notes

Overview

This exercise demonstrates how people may be resistant to change and how uncomfortable simple changes may feel.

Goals

1. To allow participants to see that they may feel uncomfortable with change.
2. To show how easy it is to have a feeling of resistance to change because it doesn't feel right.

Time required

5–10 minutes.

Size of group

Unlimited.

Material required

None.

Procedure

1. Ask the participants to stand and hold their arms straight out in front of them. Now ask them to clasp their own hands together.

2. Ask them to note which thumb is on top of their clasped hands.
3. Now ask them to reclasp their hands together, but this time with the thumb from the other hand on top.
4. Ask them to tell the person next to them how they felt when they changed the position and vice versa.
5. You can now lead into a discussion about change, how uncomfortable we may feel with change or the resistance to change.

Discussion points

1. Did people feel okay when they changed positions?
2. How many people felt uncomfortable?
3. How many people couldn't do it?

Trainer's notes

Overview
This exercise demonstrates how people may be resistant to change and how uncomfortable simple changes may feel.

Goals
1. To allow participants to see that they may feel uncomfortable with change.
2. To show how easy it is to have a feeling of resistance to change because it doesn't feel right.

Time required
5–10 minutes.

Size of goup
Unlimited.

Material required
None.

Procedure
1. Ask the participants to stand and hold their arms straight out in front of them. Now ask them to fold their own arms together.
2. Ask them to note which arm is on top.
3. Now ask them to refold their arms together, but this time with the other arm on top.
4. Ask them to tell the person next to them how they felt when they changed the position and vice versa.
5. You can now lead into a discussion about change, how uncomfortable we may feel with change or the resistance to change.

Discussion points
1. Did people feel okay when they changed positions?
2. How many people felt uncomfortable?
3. How many people couldn't do it?

Trainer's notes

80. Clowns

Overview
This is an icebreaker that could be used on the final day of a lengthy course.

Goals
1. To get the participants thinking in a positive way.
2. To allow participants to give positive personal messages to the rest of the participants.

Time required
30–60 minutes depending on the size of the group.

Size of group
Unlimited, but the larger the group the longer it will take.

Material required
A pen and a copy of the 'Reflection Card' for each participant. Each card is to have a participant's name previously placed at the top.

Procedure
1. Introduce the exercise by telling all members of the group that they will be given a copy of the 'Reflection Card' and a pen each.
2. Hand out the cards so that each participant has one. Make sure that no one has their own card to start with.
3. Now ask the participants to reflect on the past training period and think of a positive point for the person whose name appears on the card they have. When they have a positive point they are to write it down on the card and then pass the card on to another person in the group. Ensure that everyone in the group gets a chance to write on each card and that they understand that all comments *must* be positive.
4. After the cards have been passed completely around the group, give each card to the person to whom it belongs. The members of the group are now given 5 minutes to read and reflect on the comments on their own card.
5. Conclude the exercise by telling everyone to put their card in the bottom drawer back at work, and, when they are having a bad day, to take the card out and read it.

Discussion points
1. How does everyone feel?
2. Does anyone have any comments written on their cards they would like to talk about?

Variations
1. The group could sit in a circle and pass the cards around in an agreed direction.
2. You may or may not decide to participate. If you have been involved with the group from the beginning it is highly recommended that you do.

Source
Kate Chaffer, Eastwood, NSW.

Trainer's notes

Reflection Card

Name:

Overview

This exercise shows how difficult change can be.

Goals

1. To allow participants to see how they react to change.
2. To get the participants thinking about change, its implementation and its acceptance.

Time required

5–10 minutes.

Size of group

Unlimited.

Material required

A sheet of paper and a pen for each participant.

Procedure

1. Give a pen and a sheet of paper to each participant.
2. Ask participants to think about an object they have lying around somewhere at home. When they have thought of the object they are to draw it using the hand they normally don't use for writing.
3. Tell them to silently give their drawing to the person sitting beside them. This person is to guess what the object is, and write the name of the object underneath the drawing.
4. After each drawing has been labelled, it is to be handed back to the owner.
5. Tie the exercise in with the theme of change. An explanation of the exercise could be that people normally feel uncomfortable with change (using a different hand) and are uncertain of the outcome (will they know what it is?).

Discussion points

1. How many objects were guessed correctly? (Normally the majority.)
2. Who felt uncomfortable using the other hand?
3. Do we tend to resist even simple changes?
4. How can we overcome this resistance?

Variations

1. Other types of objects may be stipulated.
2. Participants may also be asked to close their eyes while drawing.

Trainer's notes

82. Come Back

Overview

This is an exercise to get participants back on time after a break.

Goals

1. To let the participants know what time they are required back after a break.
2. To ensure that the participants are back on time.

Time required

2 minutes.

Size of group

Unlimited.

Material required

None.

Procedure

1. Inform the group that they will be going on a break in a couple of minutes.

2. Before they go, ask them to synchronise their watches with yours. (Try to keep a straight face for this exercise.)
3. Now add on the length of the break time exactly and tell the group that that will be the starting time, with or without all of them. For example, if the time is 10:13 am, tell the group to synchronise watches, that they are going to have a 20-minute break and that they must be back at exactly 10:33 am.
4. Start at the designated time, even if only a few participants have arrived back. The late returns will soon get the message.

Variation

1. Let one of the participants have the responsibility of getting all of the group back at the specified time.

Source

Jude Pettitt, Lugarno, NSW.

Trainer's notes

83. Post-it

Overview
This is an alternative way to evaluate a program in place of end of course reaction sheets.

Goal
1. To allow participants to spontaneously evaluate a program.

Time required
10–20 minutes, depending on the number and type of questions.

Size of group
Up to 50.

Material required
Sufficient 'Post-it' notes, pens and prepared sheets of butcher's paper.

Procedure
1. Begin the evaluation process by telling the participants that they will be required to evaluate certain items before the close of the program.
2. Give each participant at least the same number of 'Post-it' notes as there are questions or points indicated on each sheet of butcher's paper, and a pen to write with.
3. Display the prepared sheets of butcher's paper with the questions or points you want evaluated or commented on. You could include the following questions. What did you like about the program? What would you change? What is the best thing you picked up? What barriers do you have for implementing these ideas? Messages for other course participants? And so on.
4. Ask the participants to walk around the room, read each sheet one at a time, write their comments on the 'Post-it' notes and stick them to the sheets of butcher's paper.
5. After all participants have commented on each sheet of butcher's paper, you can close the program.

Variations
1. This could be done as a team exercise where teams of 5–7 are formed and asked to put a team note on each of the sheets of butcher's paper.
2. All comments should be collated and posted out to the participants as well as being summarised in the final program report.

Source
Jude Pettitt, Lugarno, NSW.

Trainer's notes

84. 15 Pieces

Overview
This non-verbal exercise can be used effectively during a communications session.

Goal
1. To allow participants to communicate non-verbally.

Time required
30–45 minutes.

Size of group
Unlimited.

Material required
A set of 15 pieces in 5 envelopes for each 5 participants.

Procedure
1. Break the group into subgroups of 5. Any surplus members can be designated the role of observers.
2. Give each member in the subgroup an envelope containing 3 pieces of a square. Ask them not to open their envelopes yet.
3. Tell the subgroup that each member has a number of pieces in their envelope to build a square. Some of the parts however are located with other members within their subgroup. The task is for each member to complete a square. All squares are to be the same size.

4. Tell participants that this exercise is to be completed non-verbally (nothing at all is to be said), force is not to be used to gain other pieces.
5. Debrief by discussing non-verbal communication and problem-solving methods for this type of situation.

Discussion points
1. Did any subgroup think it had finished and then realise that all of its members had not completed the square?
2. Did anyone build a square that was too large and therefore stopped others from completing the task? What resulted?
3. How was information communicated? Was it effective?

Variations
1. Pieces can be painted different colours to confuse the task.
2. The participants may be told that the squares are all about 20 cm in size. This will speed up the process.

Source
Adapted from 'Broken Squares', Elizabeth M. Christopher and Larry E. Smith, *Leadership Training Through Gaming*, Nichols Publishing Co., New York, and Kogan Page Limited, London, 1987.

Trainer's notes

The Pieces

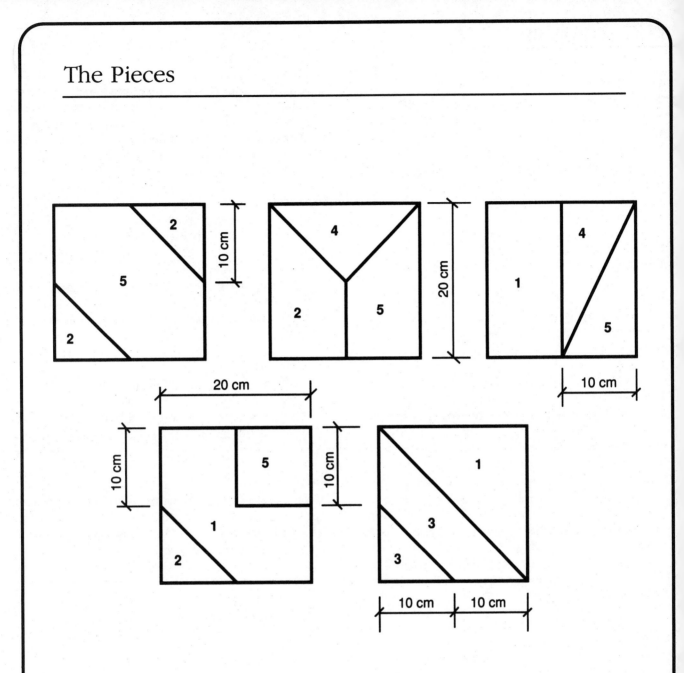

Note

All pieces marked 1 to go in envelope number 1

All pieces marked 2 to go in envelope number 2

All pieces marked 3 to go in envelope number 3

All pieces marked 4 to go in envelope number 4

All pieces marked 5 to go in envelope number 5

85. Housie

Overview
This housie game will get participants mixing.

Goal
1. To allow the participants to meet some of the other participants quickly.

Time required
15–20 minutes.

Size of group
Unlimited, preferably large (more than 20).

Material required
A housie card and a pen for each participant. Each housie card must have a matching housie number written on the back of it. A small prize is also required.

Procedure
1. Give each participant a housie card with a number written on the back of it.

2. Tell the group members that they have 10 minutes to circulate quickly among each other to get people to sign off their special number if it is included on the front of the card.
3. The person who has the most signatures at the specified time wins a prize.

Discussion points
1. Who got the most signatures?
2. How many did everyone else get?

Variation
1. Cards may be prepared to contain all of the numbers within the group. By doing this it will allow the fastest person to call 'Housie'.

Trainer's notes

Overview

This exercise allows participants to find out odd things about other group members.

Goals

1. To allow the group to get to know each other.
2. To get the group circulating.

Time required

15–20 minutes.

Size of group

Unlimited.

Material required

A 'Participant Bingo' sheet and a pen for each participant. A small prize is also required.

Procedure

1. Tell the members of the group that they are going to play 'Participant Bingo'. Give each group member a pen and a copy of the 'Participant Bingo' sheet.

2. Tell the members that they are to circulate and find people who match the requirements of each box on the sheet. When they find the person, they are to get them to write their name in the appropriate box. They then move on to find someone else. A participant is only allowed to sign one box on any sheet even though they may meet the requirements of another box.

3. The first person to complete all of the boxes is to claim the prize by calling out 'Bingo'. You check the sheet and award the prize.

Discussion points

1. Did people find out some strange things about other participants?
2. Does anyone have any questions or comments to follow up on during the next break?

Variation

1. 'Participant Bingo' sheets may be custom-made to suit the target group.

Trainer's notes

Participant Bingo

You are to find someone who:

owns a sport car	has a house in the country
is married	has 2 children
plays tennis	jogs every day
walks to work	likes reading
plays football	uses computers
races cars	scuba dives
likes knitting	enjoys fine wines
supervises staff	has 4 children
has twins	has a pet dog
has a pet cat	likes horse riding
doesn't want to be here	has blue eyes
has brown eyes	has blonde hair

87. Pick a Shape

Overview
This is a quick exercise to get participants laughing.

Goals
1. To get the participants laughing.
2. To put participants at ease.

Time required
5 minutes.

Size of group
Unlimited.

Material required
A prepared overhead projection transparency or chart.

Procedure
1. Introduce the exercise by telling the participants that they are going to be asked to associate themselves with one of the four shapes that are about to be shown.

2. Display the prepared overhead transparency and give the participants a minute to think which shape they can best associate with.
3. When everyone has selected a shape, begin by asking 'Who associated with the triangle?'. With the show of hands, tell this group of people that they have an even base and are generally fairly stable people. Then ask the people who associated with the square to show their hands. Tell them that they are solid and evenly distributed people. Ask the people who associated with the Z to raise their hands. Tell them that they are generally good leaders. Finally ask the participants who associated with the circle to show their hands. Tell them that they are preoccupied with sex and booze.
4. After the laughter stops, lead on to the topic at hand.

Variation
1. Other descriptions for the shapes may be used.

Trainer's notes

Pick a Shape

Which shape can you associate with?

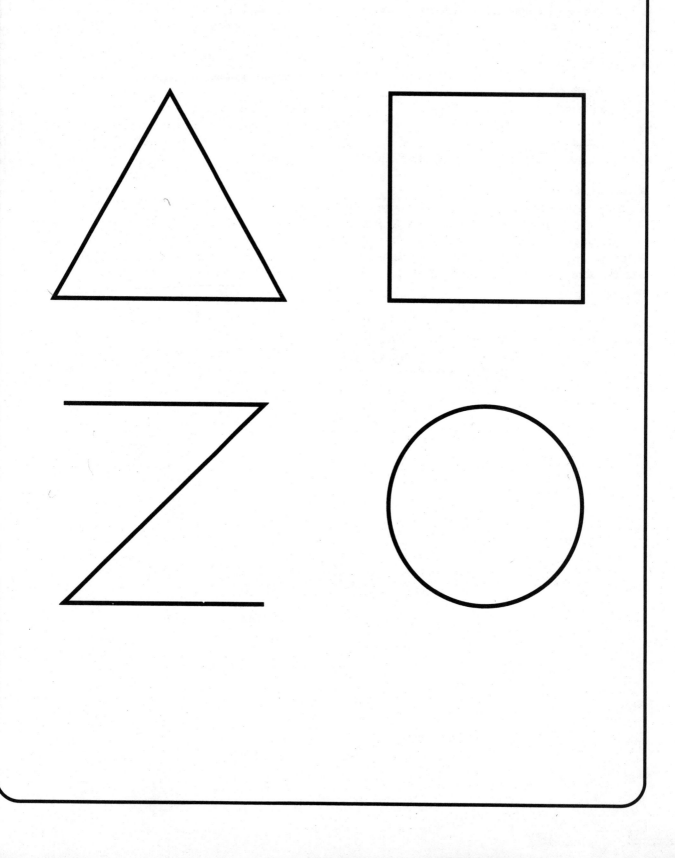

Overview

This exercise will get participants involved in simple public speaking.

Goals

1. To allow the participants the experience of talking in front of a group.
2. To see how quickly each participant can structure and control a short presentation.

Time required

30–40 minutes.

Size of group

Unlimited, but broken into groups of 5–7 participants.

Material required

A prepared list of topics, cut into separate strips, folded and placed into a small open box. Topics can include such things as cheese, coffee, pencils, computers, motor vehicles, carpet, wool, shoes, toes, fingers, tables, chairs, paper, air, water, glass, time, etc.

Procedure

1. Ask the large group to break into smaller groups of 5–7 people. Tell them that they are going to give a standing 2-minute presentation to the rest of their group.
2. Then ask the first speakers to come forward and pick a topic from the box.
3. After the speakers have selected their topics, they go back to their groups and give a 2-minute impromptu talk. This process continues for all of the participants.
4. After all participants have given their 2-minute impromptu talk debrief the whole exercise.

Discussion points

1. How many people felt extremely threatened?
2. How much preparation is required for a short presentation?
3. Do people want to do it again?

Variations

1. You could allow the participants to select their own topics.
2. The exercise can be done using one large group as long as time is available.

Trainer's notes

89. Where Did It Go?

Overview
This exercise allows participants to see the importance of setting priorities on tasks.

Goals
1. To allow participants to see where their time goes.
2. To let participants see that they must set priorities on tasks and projects.

Time required
40–60 minutes.

Size of group
Unlimited.

Material required
A copy of the 'Yesterday' handout and a pen for each participant.

Procedure
1. Introduce the exercise by telling the participants that they are to recall everything they did yesterday, for the whole 24 hours. Give everyone a pen and a copy of the 'Yesterday' handout.
2. Now give them 10 minutes to think about what they did yesterday and to write it down. What they write down must total 24 hours.
3. After everything has been written down, ask them to indicate a priority for each item. It can be marked as an 'A', 'B' or 'C' priority. An 'A' indicates it is linked to a major life goal or a person's top priorities. A 'B' indicates that it is something that has to be done, but it isn't linked to major life goals. A 'C' indicates that it is something that could be put off for a while or perhaps didn't need to be done by the person in the first place.
4. After the list has been completed, ask how many people spent any time on their 'A' priorities. A discussion should follow, highlighting the importance of working on 'A' priorities every day, and getting rid of most of the 'C' priorities.

Discussion points
1. Who spent most of their time on 'C' priorities?
2. Who spent most of their time on 'B' priorities?
3. Who spent most of their time on 'A' priorities?
4. How important are each of these groups?
5. Do people have a balance of time between business and personal time?
6. Could people recall everything they did yesterday? If not, is it possible that the time used wasn't that productive?
7. Is relaxation time an 'A' priority?

Variation
1. A time log can be used prior to the program.

Trainer's notes

Yesterday

Task	Time	Priority

Total time spent on 'A' tasks =

Total time spent on 'B' tasks =

Total time spent on 'C' tasks =

90. Post Me a Note

ITCES

Overview
This icebreaker could be used on the final day of a lengthy course.

Goals
1. To get the participants thinking in a positive way.
2. To allow participants to give positive personal messages to the rest of the participants.

Time required
30–60 minutes depending on the size of the group.

Size of group
Unlimited, but the larger the group the longer it will take.

Material required
A pen and a large envelope for each participant. Numerous strips of paper will also be required.

Procedure
1. Tell the participants that they are going to be involved in a positive reflection exercise. Ask them to move their chairs so that they will form a large circle.
2. Give each participant a pen, an envelope and enough strips of paper to write one comment per person in the group. Ask them to write their own name on the front of the envelope.
3. Then ask them to give the envelope to the person sitting on their right. Tell this person to think of a nice or positive point about the person whose name appears on the envelope, write it on a strip of paper and put it into the envelope. The envelope is then passed on to the person on their right, and so on. Ensure that everyone understands that all written comments are to be positive.
4. When the envelopes have completed the full circle, tell participants they may go through their own envelope and read the comments. They should take these positive thoughts away with them.

Discussion points
1. How does everyone feel?
2. Does anyone have any comments in their envelope they would like to talk about?

Variations
1. Give each participant a sheet of butcher's paper at the end of the exercise to paste the strips of paper on. This can be kept as a permanent reference to look at when they are feeling a little down.
2. The facilitator may or may not decide to participate. If you have been involved with the group from the beginning it is highly recommended that you do.

Source
Adapted from a suggestion by Georgina Rea, Lakemba, NSW.

Trainer's notes

91. Spider's Web

Overview
This exercise can be used to conclude a lengthy program. It should be used with participants who have spent a lot of time together.

Goals
1. To allow participants to pass on final messages to the whole group.
2. To encourage future networking among participants.

Time required
30–60 minutes depending on the number of participants.

Size of group
Up to 30.

Material required
A large ball of wool or string.

Procedure
1. Ask the members of the group to stand and form a tight circle.

2. Start the spider's web by passing on your final comments to the group. You may say things about what you've received from the program, what you hope to see happen in the future with the new information given, etc. After you have said your bit, hold the ball by the loose end and throw the ball to a participant across the circle.
3. The receiver gives a final message to the rest of the group and then throws the ball to another group member while holding on to the loose piece of string. This process continues until all participants have had a chance to speak. At the conclusion all participants should be holding the string or wool and it should have formed something similar in shape to an abstract spider's web.

Source
Jude Pettitt, Lugarno, NSW.

Trainer's notes

92. Personally

Overview
This is a simple way to formally conclude a program.

Goal
1. To allow the participants to state what they feel they gained from the program.

Time required
15–20 minutes.

Size of group
Unlimited.

Material required
None.

Procedure
1. Ask the group to break up into pairs. Ask them to complete the following statement to their partner. 'Personally, one thing I gained from this program was ...'

2. After the individuals have answered each other, you can go around the whole group getting a quick response from everyone on the question.

Discussion points
1. Is all of the feedback positive?
2. Does anyone have anything else they would like to add after hearing everyone else?

Variation
1. If the group is not too large, you can ask the question of everyone in the group without breaking into pairs.

Trainer's notes

93. The Application

Overview
This exercise will allow participants to think about ways they can implement the new knowledge, skills or attitudes back in the workplace.

Goals
1. To get participants to think about ways of implementing the training back in the workplace.
2. To formally conclude a training program.

Time required
15–20 minutes.

Size of group
Unlimited.

Material required
None.

Procedure
1. Break the group into pairs. Get them to ask each other the following question: 'How are you going to implement this training back in the workplace?'.

2. After all participants have answered their partner's question, you can go around the group getting a quick response from everyone. If anyone has any barriers or problems with implementing the training, ask them why and follow this up with a brainstorming session for possible solutions.

Discussion points
1. Can everyone apply the new knowledge, skills or attitudes back in the workplace?
2. Does anyone have a problem with the implementation?
3. How will the rest of the employees in the participants' areas feel about the change?

Variation
1. Get everyone to write their response to the question on a piece of paper, collect the pieces and then read them out.

Trainer's notes

94. Clap

Overview
This is a mid-course energiser to get your participants moving and laughing.

Goals
1. To get participants clapping and moving around.
2. To get participants laughing.

Time required
2–5 minutes.

Size of group
Unlimited.

Material required
None.

Procedure
1. Tell the members of the group that they are going to be involved in a mid-course exercise. Tell them performing this exercise is a custom that goes back for many programs.

2. Now tell them that the custom is for them to applaud the person who provided the tea-making facilities (or anything the facilitator selects). After this round of applause, tell the group about the second part of the ritual. They are now to applaud the person who cleans up the training room (or anyone else the facilitator selects). This can go on for as long as you wish.
3. Encourage loud applause to commence with, and build up to standing, cheering, stamping and whistling.

Discussion point
1. Does anyone else have a nominee for applause?

Variations
1. The facilitator can select group members for the applause.
2. A 'Clap Meter' can be drawn on the whiteboard for participants to see how their applause rates.

Trainer's notes

95. Time Line

Overview

This exercise will allow participants to become more familiar with each other's feelings. It can also be used to assess stress levels in the participants' lives.

Goals

1. To allow participants to identify 6 major changes in their lives.
2. To allow participants to map those changes out and to talk about them if they wish to.

Time required

15 minutes.

Size of group

Unlimited.

Material required

A sheet of paper and a pen for each participant.

Procedure

1. Give each member a sheet of paper and a pen. Ask them to identify 6 major changes in their lives that they can recall. Also tell the participants that they will not be required to state what all of these events are, they will however be asked to share one of them with a partner.
2. When they have thought of these life changes, tell them to draw a time line starting at the first major event and finishing now. Along the time line they are to mark in the changes. They are not required to write what these events are.
3. When the 6 events are marked, ask them to turn to a partner and tell them what one of the events is. After both have described their event, ask them to indicate what feelings they had before, during and after this major life change.
4. Now lead the discussion in the topic area.

Discussion points

1. Did anyone have the majority of these events grouped together?
2. Can we use something like this time line to identify people who are highly stressed?

Variation

1. You can ask that the time line start from the age of 1, 5, 10 or 20 years or even start at birth.

Trainer's notes

96. Orientation Quiz

Overview
This is a quiz to be used before induction or orientation programs.

Goals
1. To get participants mixing with each other.
2. To increase the participants' curiosity.

Time required
15–30 minutes depending on the length of the quiz.

Size of group
Unlimited.

Material required
A copy of a quiz and a pen for each participant. You must prepare the quiz before the program commences. It should be based on interesting facts about the organisation and the people involved in it. All of the quiz questions should be on a positive note and should be interesting to the participants.

Procedure
1. Tell the members of the group that they are going to be given a quiz. Give each person a copy of the quiz and a pen. They are allowed 10–15 minutes to answer as many questions as possible. The answers should be able to be found from the other group members.
2. After time has been called, get the participants to swap papers and then read them out the right answers. Give the person with the highest score a prize.

Discussion points
1. Did anyone know all the answers to start with?
2. Did anyone find someone who knows a lot about a particular area?

Variations
1. The group can be broken into teams of 5–7 people and the team that scores the highest wins the prize.
2. A quiz can be used for any other session or program.

Trainer's notes

Overview

This exercise allows participants to use trivia and to find out odd things about other group members.

Goals

1. To allow members of the group to get to know each other.
2. To get the group circulating.

Time required

15–20 minutes.

Size of group

Unlimited.

Material required

A 'People Scavenger' sheet and a pen for each participant. A small prize is also required.

Procedure

1. Tell the group members that they are going to play 'People Scavenger'. Give each member a pen and a copy of the 'People Scavenger' sheet.

2. Tell the members they are to circulate and find people who match the requirements of each box on the sheet. When they find the person, they are to get them to write their name in the appropriate box. They then move on to find someone else. A participant is only allowed to sign one box on any sheet even though they may meet the requirements of another box. The first person to complete all of the boxes claims the prize by calling out, 'I'm the best scavenger'. Check the sheet and award the prize.

Discussion points

1. Did people find out some strange things about other participants?
2. Does anyone have any questions or comments to follow up during the next break?

Variation

1. 'People Scavenger' sheets may be custom-made to suit the target group.

Trainer's notes

People Scavenger

You are to find someone who:

has the same zodiac sign as yours	is a supervisor
has worked here for 1 year	knows how many cars are in the car park
has worked here for more than 10 years	has worked here before
is a manager	knows how many words are on a twenty dollar note
has the same name as yours	uses the credit union
catches the same train as you	lives in the same suburb as you
knows how many times the word express is shown on the American Express card	drives to work
has a university qualification	knows how many 5s are on a five dollar note
knows when the company started	knows the boss's middle name

ITCMP

Overview

This exercise emphasises why people should work together.

Goal

1. To allow participants to see how they can achieve more goals if they work together rather than compete with each other.

Time required

5 minutes.

Size of group

Unlimited.

Material required

None.

Procedure

1. Ask the members of the group to stand and form pairs.
2. Tell the pairs to face each other and to hold their partner's right hand with their own right hand. This will be similar to a handshake.
3. Now tell them to make as many wishes as they possibly can in the next 60 seconds, while still holding on to their partner's hand.
4. After the 60 seconds, tell them that they will be granted one of their wishes each time they can touch their right hip with their right hand (while still holding onto their partner). They now have 60 seconds to have as many wishes granted as they can.
5. At the end of this 60-second period, ask how many pairs didn't have any wishes granted between them. Then ask the group how many pairs had between 1 and 5 wishes granted. Finally ask how many pairs had all of their wishes granted, plus some to spare.
6. Then you should ask a pair from each category to demonstrate how they tried to gain their wishes. Start with the 0 scores and work up to the higher scores. By demonstrating this way, the group will be able to see how the pairs that co-operated got far more wishes granted than those who didn't.

Discussion points

1. Why was it that some pairs didn't have any wishes granted?
2. Are we all naturally competitive? Why?
3. Can we change this behaviour?
4. How can we co-operate?

Variation

1. Have all of the participants close their eyes or have them blindfolded.

Trainer's notes

99. Paper Planes

Overview
With this activity participants can compare organisation and task complexity.

Goal
1. To allow participants to look at their organisational and production abilities in a non-threatening exercise.

Time required
60–90 minutes.

Size of group
12–32 participants, broken into 2–4 teams of 5–7 members with at least 1 observer for each group.

Material required
A stopwatch and approximately 100 sheets of paper for each team. Used A4 sheets of paper cut in half will be suitable.

Procedure
1. Tell the group that it is going to be broken into teams and involved in a competitive exercise. Form teams with 5–7 participants. You need at least 1 observer for each team. Tell the teams the exercise will involve each team in building a prototype paper plane for evaluation against the other teams' planes, the selection of the most suitable model for construction, the mass production of the selected model including financial projections and the final comparison between groups to see who made the greatest profit.
2. Give each team 10 sheets of paper. Ask them to construct a paper plane that will fly across the room and that also looks aesthetically pleasing. After the members within the team agree on the final model, they are to construct enough identical models so that each other team may have one.
3. When all teams have finished building their prototypes, each team gets 1 set of prototype planes. The whole group now votes on which plane is the best design, based on practicality of manufacture and its final appearance.
4. Once the final design has been selected collect all materials back from the teams. Tell the teams they will now be given 10 minutes to forecast how many paper planes they can build in a 10-minute period and how much profit they can make. They will be charged for both materials and for time used. The planes must be of the same quality as the prototype and will be examined on completion

by the customer. They must pass this examination to be counted. The costs are shown below.
5. Give the teams 10 minutes to plan. During this time you brief the observers. They are to note whatever you request (probably interaction, roles, task breakdown, and conflict). They are also the official time-keepers. Also tell the observers that after the construction phase, they will become the customer. As the customer they will have the final say as to whether each plane will be accepted or rejected.
6. Give the teams 10 minutes to construct their paper planes. Then the customer for each team evaluates the planes. At the end of this phase each team calculates its final profit or loss.
7. All results are compared, and the winning team announced. Feedback is obtained from the team members and from the observers in the identified areas.
8. You can now lead the discussion on the topic.

Discussion points
1. Was the final result different from the forecast? Why?
2. Was there any conflict in the group?
3. Did certain people take on or accept roles within the team?
4. Was quality a concern?
5. Did everyone participate in the discussion and decision-making process?

Variations
1. A set of colouring pencils may be given to each group at the beginning with the initial 10 sheets of paper.
2. An additional step may be included. The teams are given larger sheets of paper along with a pair of scissors. They are then also required to cut out the specified shape and size as part of the production process.

Costs
$1.00 for each sheet of paper.
$10.00 for each minute of time taken during construction.

Potential income
$5.00 per completed plane (must be passed by customer).

100. Agenda

Overview
This exercise will allow the group to construct its own agenda for a team-building session.

Goals
1. To allow the group members to get to know each other a little better.
2. To allow the group to select agenda items for discussion.
3. To allow the group to rank the agenda items for discussion.
4. To encourage ownership of the agenda items and commitment to them.

Time required
40–60 minutes.

Size of group
Unlimited, but all members should be from the same work group.

Material required
A pen and paper for each participant and a flipchart and marker.

Procedure
1. Break the group members into pairs. Ask them to pair up with someone they haven't spoken to recently, if possible.
2. Tell them that they will have 5 minutes to interview each other about their work and items they would like to see included on the agenda for discussion.
3. After the interviews have finished, the group should be seated again so that all members can see each other. Now ask the pairs to repeat their partner's suggested agenda items one at a time.

The partner who is having their items being repeated by the other person may clarify or add any points they want. As agenda items are being raised, you should list them on the flipchart paper.
4. When everyone has finished, give them a pen and paper. Ask each individual to identify their top 3 items. When the participants have completed this phase, get the information from them and mark the 3 items on the flipchart by placing a tick beside the item. Place the items with the greatest number of ticks on another flipchart.
5. Now ask the participants to rank these final agenda items in order of importance. After the individual ranking has been completed, get the information from the participants one at a time and collate it on the flipchart.
6. When all of the items have been rank ordered, the group may start discussing the items from the top. This will ensure the important items are covered. The lower ranking items may be covered if time permits.

Note: Outstanding items can be carried over. Ensure that none of the participants feel that their agenda items not covered were more important than those covered. Make sure that all people are involved in the discussions and that correct meeting techniques are used.

Discussion points
1. Was this a practical way to ensure the important agenda items were discussed?
2. Are there any items that weren't covered that should have been?

Variation
1. One of the participants can be briefed to lead the exercise or just the discussions.

Trainer's notes

SAMPLE OBSERVER'S SHEETS

The attached 'Observer's Sheets' are to be used as sample designs. They have been included as references for you to design your own 'Observer's Sheets'. It is important that anytime you do use observers, that they know exactly what it is they are supposed to be observing.

By using a properly designed observation sheet you are ensuring consistency. You are also ensuring that all of the points you wanted raised will be covered in the final discussion phase.

Observer's Sheet No. 1

It is your task to record what happens in chronological order. Record the time i[...] the left-hand column, what the observation was in the centre column, and wh[...] was involved in the third column.

Do not take part in the exercise or pass any comment or make any suggesti[...] The information you will be providing after the exercise will assist the wh[...] group learn about points which are directly relevant to the way in which [...] operate.

Time	Observation	Name

Observer's Sheet No. 2

It is your task to record appropriate points under the headings listed below.
Do not take part in the exercise or pass any comment or make any suggestion. The information you will be providing after the exercise will assist the whole group learn about points which are directly relevant to the way in which they operate.

Was the exercise planned?

How was it planned?

Were people organised?

Were objectives set?

Observer's Sheet No. 3

It is your task to record appropriate points under the headings listed below.
Do not take part in the exercise or pass any comment or make any suggestion. The information you will be providing after the exercise will assist the whole group learn about points which are directly relevant to the way in which they operate.

How was the exercise analysed?

Were people organised?

Were objectives set?

Were things properly delegated?

Were all available resources used?

How was the group lead?

Were problems solved?

How effective was the communication?

How were alternatives discussed and evaluated?

What else was worth recording?

Observer's Sheet No. 1

It is your task to record what happens in chronological order. Record the time in the left-hand column, what the observation was in the centre column, and who was involved in the third column.

Do not take part in the exercise or pass any comment or make any suggestion. The information you will be providing after the exercise will assist the whole group learn about points which are directly relevant to the way in which they operate.

Time	Observation	Name

Observer's Sheet No. 2

It is your task to record appropriate points under the headings listed below.

Do not take part in the exercise or pass any comment or make any suggestion. The information you will be providing after the exercise will assist the whole group learn about points which are directly relevant to the way in which they operate.

Was the exercise planned?

How was it planned?

Were people organised?

Were objectives set?

Were all available resources used?

Was the time controlled?

How was the group led?

What roles did people take?

How effective was the communication?

What else was worth recording?

Observer's Sheet No. 3

It is your task to record appropriate points under the headings listed below.

Do not take part in the exercise or pass any comment or make any suggestion. The information you will be providing after the exercise will assist the whole group learn about points which are directly relevant to the way in which they operate.

How was the exercise analysed?

Were people organised?

Were objectives set?

Were things properly delegated?

Were all available resources used?

How was the group lead?

Were problems solved?

How effective was the communication?

How were alternatives discussed and evaluated?

What else was worth recording?

BIBLIOGRAPHY AND OTHER REFERENCES

The symbols to the left of the title have been included to give the reader a guide as to the usefulness of these books. The key to the symbols is shown below.

Reference key
❂   Read this one and put it in your library, it's good.
☆   Read this if you're interested enough.
★   Read this if you've got nothing else to do.

★ BADDELEY, Alan, *Your Memory: A User's Guide*, Penguin Books, England, 1983.

☆ BAKER, Pat, MARSHALL, Mary-Ruth, *More Simulation Games*, The Joint Board of Christian Education of Australia and New Zealand, Melbourne, 1977.

☆ ——, *Using Simulation Games*, 2nd Edition, The Joint Board of Christian Education of Australia and New Zealand, Melbourne, 1982.

☆ CARRIER, Michael, *Take 5: Games and Activities for the Language Learner*, Harrap Limited, London, 1983.

❂ CHRISTOPHER, Elizabeth M., SMITH, Larry E., *Leadership Training through Gaming*, Nichols Publishing Co., New York, and Kogan Page Limited, London, 1987.

★ EITINGTON, Julius E., *The Winning Trainer*, Gulf Publishing Company, Texas, 1984.

★ ELLINGTON, Henry, ADDINALL, Eric, PERCIVAL, Fred, *A Handbook of Game Design*, Kogan Page Limited, London, 1982.

★ ——, *Case Studies in Game Design*, Kogan Page Limited, London, 1984.

★ *ELT Documents: Games, Simulations and Role-Playing*, The British Council English Teaching Information Centre, London, 1977.

☆ FLUEGELMAN, Andrew (ed.), *More New Games*, Doubleday, New York, 1981.

☆ ——, *The New Games Book*, Doubleday, New York, 1976.

❂ FORBESS-GREENE, Sue, *The Encyclopedia of Icebreakers*, University Associates, California, 1983.

❂ KROEHNERT, Gary, *Basic Training for Trainers*, McGraw-Hill Book Company Australia, Sydney, 1990.

☆ MILL, Cyril R., *Activities for Trainers: 50 Useful Designs*, University Associates, California, 1980.

❂ NEWSTROM, John W., SCANNELL, Edward E., *Games Trainers Play*, McGraw-Hill, Inc., New York, 1980.

★ *Oddities in Words, Pictures and Figures*, Reader's Digest Services Pty Limited, Sydney, 1975.

★ ORLICK, Terry, *The Cooperative Sports and Games Book*, Pantheon Books, Canada, 1978.

★ ——, *The Second Cooperative Sports and Games Book*, Pantheon Books, Canada, 1982.

❂ PFEIFFER, J. William, JONES, John E., *A Handbook of Structured Experiences for Human Relations Training*, Volumes 1–10, University Associates, California, 1975–85.

☆ ROHNKE, Karl, *Cowstails and Cobras II*, Kendall/Hunt Publishing Company, Iowa, 1989.

☆ ——, *Silver Bullets*, Kendall/Hunt Publishing Company, Iowa, 1984.

❂ SCANNELL, Edward E., NEWSTROM, John W., *More Games Trainers Play*, McGraw-Hill, Inc., New York, 1983.

☆ TUBESING, Nancy Loving, TUBESING, Donald A., *Structured Exercises in Stress Management*, Volumes 1 and 2, Whole Person Press, Duluth MN, 1983.

☆ ——, *Structured Exercises in Wellness Promotion*, Volumes 1 and 2, Whole Person Press, Duluth MN, 1983.

★ VAN MENTS, Morry, *The Effective Use of Role-Play*, Kogan Page Limited, London, 1983.

❂ WOODCOCK, Mike, *50 Activities for Teambuilding*, Gower Publishing Company, England, 1989.

★ WRIGHT, Andrew, BETTERIDGE, David, BUCKBY, Michael, *Games for Language Learning*, Cambridge University Press, Cambridge, 1979.

35. 3-Minute Test

Overview
This quick quiz tests how well participants follow written communication.

Goal
1. To develop skills in communication.

Time required
10 minutes.

Size of group
Unlimited.

Material required
A copy of the '3-Minute Test' and a pen for each participant.

Procedure
1. After an introduction to the topic of communication, inform the group that they are going to be given a 3-minute test in communication. They are to use test conditions. You should also ask that if anyone has sat this test previously they should still participate, but remember the test conditions.
2. Place a pen and a copy of the '3-Minute Test' face down in front of each participant. Tell them that as soon as the timing commences they will have exactly 3 minutes to complete the quiz.
3. When it has been completed, lead a discussion on the giving and receiving of communication.

Discussion points
1. Who followed the instructions?
2. Who only has their name written in the top right-hand corner?
3. How do the participants feel who followed all instructions except the first?

Variation
1. Some questions may be modified to suit the work environment or subject matter.

Trainer's notes

3-Minute Test

or

How well do you receive communication?

___

1. Read everything before doing anything.
2. Print your name in the upper right-hand corner of this paper.
3. Circle the word 'name' in sentence two.
4. Draw five small squares in the upper left-hand corner of this paper.
5. Call your name aloud.
6. Write your name again under the second title of this paper.
7. After the first title write 'Yes', 'Yes', 'Yes'.
8. Draw a circle around sentence five.
9. Put an 'X' in the lower left-hand corner of this paper.
10. If you are enjoying this test say 'Yes', if not say 'No'.
11. Loudly call out your last name when you reach this point in the test.
12. On the right margin of this paper, multiply 66 by 7.
13. Draw a rectangle around the word 'paper' in sentence number four.
14. If you think you have followed directions carefully to this point, call 'I have'.
15. On the left margin of this paper add 69 and 98.
16. Count in your normal speaking voice from 10 to 1 backwards.
17. Stand up, turn around once and sit down.
18. Say out loud, 'I am nearly finished, I have followed directions'.
19. If you are the first to this point say, 'I am the leader in following directions'.
20. Now that you have finished reading carefully, as instructed in sentence 1, do only sentence number 2.

36. Pass the Microphone

CF

Overview
This technique can be used to control small group discussion.

Goals
1. To allow group members to all participate in a small group discussion.
2. To let the group see that group discussion can be relatively easy to control on controversial topics.

Time required
As long as required.

Size of group
6–12.

Material required
An object to be used as an imaginary microphone.

Procedure
1. Inform the group members that they are about to participate in a group discussion on a controversial topic you select.
2. Get the group members to sit in a circle, either in their chairs or sitting on the floor. If you prefer them to sit on the floor try to have plenty of cushions for them to sit on.
3. Let them know that the object you are about to place in the middle of the circle is a microphone and that if they wish to speak they must hold the microphone. Participants are not permitted to speak unless they hold the microphone.
4. When they finish speaking or giving their point of view they are to place the microphone back in the middle of the circle for the next speaker to pick up and use.
5. Should you notice that any of the participants are a little backward in reaching for the microphone, you have the power to hand the microphone to any of them. No other group member has this power.
6. Finish the discussion as input starts to diminish and then debrief the exercise.

Discussion points
1. Did everyone get a chance to have uninterrupted input when they wanted?
2. Are the introverts and extroverts made more even with an exercise like this?

Variations
1. Put a time limit on how long a participant can hold the microphone on any given occasion.
2. If there are identified participants who are regarded as too dominant the facilitator may decide to limit the number of times each participant may use the microphone.

Trainer's notes

37. The Watch Face

Overview

Participants get a chance to see that they may not be as observant as they think they are.

Goals

1. To let participants see how unobservant they are.
2. To make participants aware that they may take too many things for granted.

Time required

5 minutes.

Size of group

Unlimited.

Material required

A participant's watch.

Procedure

1. When you are ready to commence this exercise ask a volunteer for the loan of a watch.
2. With the watch hidden from the owner, ask the owner to describe the watch accurately to the group.

3. After the description is given, ask the owner specific questions about the watch. These questions could include the following. Does the watch face have numbers, roman numerals, symbols or blank spaces? Are the numbers located on the inside or outside of the minute markings? Where is the brand name printed on the watch face? Are the hands straight or are they shaped?
4. Give the watch back to the participant and debrief the exercise.

Note: This exercise works best if the facilitator only lets volunteers hand over watches with hands.

Discussion points

1. How is it that participants couldn't describe an item that they look at dozens of times each day?
2. How can we improve our observation techniques?

Variation

1. Get more than one watch and repeat the exercise to prove the point.

Trainer's notes

Overview

This simple exercise shows participants how to relax themselves.

Goal

1. To show participants how to use a relaxation technique.

Time required

10 minutes.

Size of group

Unlimited.

Material required

None.

Procedure

1. Use this exercise after a session on stress management or relaxation techniques. Tell the participants that they are going to participate in a relaxation exercise. Make sure that none of the participants suffer from dizzy spells or breathing problems before they begin this exercise.
2. Tell the participants to sit comfortably, close their eyes and listen to your instructions.
3. Now read the group the following. 'Concentrate all of your thoughts into your right arm, stretch your arm out straight in front of you and make a tense fist and tense all of the other muscles in your arm as well. As you do this take a deep breath and say to yourself "Let". Breathe out slowly after about five seconds and say to yourself "go". Place your arm slowly down by your side and feel it relax completely.'
4. Follow the same procedure for the left arm, the right leg, the left leg, the back muscles, the neck and lastly the face muscles.

Discussion points

1. Did it work?
2. How do you feel now?
3. Can this technique be used at both home and work?

Variations

1. A prerecorded tape may be used to give the participants the main relaxation instructions.
2. Soft, slow background music may be used to improve the results.

Trainer's notes

39. Note to Me

Overview
This exercise shows a method of course follow-up.

Goals
1. To get the participants to identify ways of using this training back in the workplace.
2. To let participants know that any training should have some form of follow-up.

Time required
20 minutes.

Size of group
Unlimited.

Material required
A sheet of blank paper, a pen and an envelope for each participant.

Procedure
1. Tell the participants that they are going to write a letter to themselves about the training they have just been involved in. Give each participant a pen, a blank sheet of paper and an envelope.

2. They are to identify ways of implementing this training back in the workplace, and then list these ideas on the sheet of paper in the form of a reminder note to themselves. They should also write down any foreseeable problems and solutions in the implementation of this training.
3. When they have finished writing their notes out, tell them to address the envelope to themselves, put the letter inside it and seal it.
4. Collect the sealed envelopes. You are now responsible for posting these letters out to the participants after an agreed time, normally 3 to 6 months.

Discussion points
1. Will the plan be modified back in the workplace?
2. What will everyone do if they get this letter and the implementation hasn't been successful?

Variations
1. You can have a prepared printed sheet for the participants to use.
2. Have participants pair up and write each other's letter.

Trainer's notes